Quick Guide to NetWare

for the Systems Administrator

Carolyn Jorgensen

In collaboration with Dennis Bowman

Brady

New York
Sydney

London
Tokyo

Toronto
Singapore

BRADY

Simon & Schuster, Inc.
15 Columbus Circle
New York, NY 10023

Distributed by Prentice Hall Trade

Manufactured in the United States of America

1 2 3 4 5 6 7 8 9 10

Library of Congress Cataloging-in-Publication Data

Jorgensen, Carolyn.
Quick guide to NetWare for the system administrator / Carolyn Jorgensen.
p. cm.
ISBN 0-13-199977-X
1. NetWare (Computer operating system) I. Title.
QA76.76.063J67 1990
650'028'5571369—dc20 89-77372
CIP

Limits of Liability and Disclaimer of Warranty

Trademarks

Acknowledgments

This book would not have been possible without the help of many people. First of all, I would like to recognize the employees of the Morris Management Company, especially Mark Spencer for the opportunity of working with a great group of users.

Tracy Currie of McKesson Corporation helped greatly in analyzing the content and structure of this book. He patiently made his high-level expertise available despite a real time shortage in his busy schedule.

Thanks also to Pat Corrigan for his early NetWare training class and continuing support. Costa Distributing's telephone technical support division also was there when I had numerous onsite problems. Andy Jong of Winner's Circle and Larry Schmeling, Aim Systems, provided hardware for this project.

Novell deserves gratitude for their technical reviews, especially Mike Astie. Their input, assistance, and expertise is an invaluable contribution to this book.

The Finot Group, Consumers Software, Cybertek LAN Software, Inc., and Microcom Software contributed to this book by providing review copies of their software KeepTrack Plus, NetWork Courier, Network Assistant Plus, and Carbon Copy Plus, respectively.

I am grateful to the helpful staff of Brady Books who acquired, prepared, and produced this book: Laura McKenna, Susan Hunt, and Ozzievelt Owens. Special thanks to Susan Hunt, who arranged the technical reviews from Novell.

Thanks also to consultant Ralph Jenkins for his insight into NetWare 386 and the list of training centers he provided for Appendix A at the last minute. Judy Wofford did word processing and photocopying on this book.

And finally to Rick Nielson, my friend and agent, who has always been there for moral support, advice, and understanding when I needed him: thanks for your confidence.

Dedication

To my husband Gilles Estines-Ballandras with love, and to my friend and client Dennis Covington with great respect and admiration.

Contents

Part I

Exploring Your Novell Network

Chapter 1

Introduction

A systems administrator should know what the benefits of the Novell NetWare are; yet many systems administrators come from microcomputer backgrounds and they don't know how to take advantage of the power of a network. A systems administrator's job is to tailor the system to the company's resources — its people, equipment, and information. Before the systems administrator can do this, however, he or she must understand the benefits and capabilities of the network. This book will give you the information you need to manage your Novell NetWare network efficiently and use its resources to the fullest.

Who This Book Is For

This book was written for both parties who use the network, the systems administrator and the intermediate user. Often the systems administrator doesn't know how to begin learning about the system. This book will guide you through the steps you take in getting to know any network. Unlike courses in system administration, which stress the use of basic commands and don't tell you how to manage your system effectively, this book offers you a practical and organized approach.

Intermediate users treat the network as they would any computer system — seldom do they have the time to learn about the network's powerful resource management. Often they are intimidated by the mystery of the network and don't want to use the file server for fear they may make a mistake and bring down the system. They don't realize that the system is protected automatically by a security system controlled by the administrator, or that the file server reserves space for shared applications that they can use without risk to the system. Instead of copying their files to the file server shared directory space, many end users copy their files on floppy disks and send or carry them to their co-workers. This book teaches the end user how to use the file server and other resources efficiently and comfortably.

Troubleshooting is another useful topic covered in this book. When a problem occurs on the network, most people don't know where to start looking for its origin. For example, when a printer stops working most people blame the network, when the cause might really be a loose connection, a malfunctioning stand-alone computer, or cable damage. This book teaches you how to document a system so you'll know where to look when trouble starts.

If you have already taken Novell's systems administration course, this book offers you a comprehensive guide to the commands and tasks you have already learned, whether you are an administrator or an end user. If you have not taken the course, this book will teach you the basic tasks and commands required to manage it efficiently, and how to explore your system without risk. (For a list of authorized training centers that offer Novell's system administration course, see Appendix A.)

What You Should Know Before You Read This Book

This book assumes you are familiar with DOS and have confidence in performing simple DOS tasks such as copying, moving, listing, and erasing files, creating and managing subdirectory structures, and printing to different output devices with the DOS LPT1 and COM1 output ports. *DOS: Fast Access* is an excellent guide if you need a quick review of DOS commands.

It also assumes you understand the basic network components terminology such as workstation, file server, cable connection devices, and network operation system, although a quick review of each term is provided when appropriate. The assumption is made that the systems administrator is proficient at logging into his or her own network as both a user and supervisor. He or she should be able to locate, either alone or with the systems consultant, the basic components (workstations, file server, network printers) of his or her network.

About This Book

The introduction of this book focuses on the benefits of using a network system. It includes a section on version comparison and an in-depth look at the special features of the Novell NetWare system. The introduction also compares the systems administrator's duties with those of a system specialist or consultant. After you've reviewed this introduction, you will be ready to explore your own network in Chapter 2 of the book.

Chapter 2 is a hands-on tutorial to help you understand and document your Novell NetWare system. Part II, which includes Chapters 3 and 4, is a set of tasks and the commands to help you accomplish each task. These tasks include adding new users, managing the network printers, and controlling security. Users already familiar with a network can refer to the listing of NetWare tasks at the beginning of Part II. This listing shows you how to perform routine functions such as logging into the network, error handling, file and network resource management, and printing. Chapter 5 in Part III gives the systems administrator or other technical person step-by-step instructions for adding a new workstation or moving an existing one on the network. Remote connectivity to a network using a modem is the subject of Chapter 6.

Appendix A offers training and suppport information; Appendix B is a table of contents used to document your system and collection of useful forms for administering and documenting your network.

The Benefits of Using a Network

The biggest advantage of using a network is cost-effectiveness. With a network, a company doesn't have to invest in large amounts of hardware and software. Instead, hard disks, printers, applications software, and other peripherals are shared among workstations. Speed is another advantage. Thanks to its multiuser and multitasking architecture, NetWare software can perform many operations simultaneously, which means you can complete tasks faster than you could with many other systems.

Efficiency and performance is also increased on a network. Database applications, the most widely used business software, are easier to manage on a NetWare network. You get faster response times and disk access from the microcomputers on a network than you do from a stand-alone microcomputer. There are five major features built into NetWare that increase speed on the network. The features are:

1. **Distributed processing:** Each workstation runs its own applications. Data requested from the file server is downloaded to the workstation's memory and processed locally, rather than back and forth from the network.
2. **Directory caching:** The file server's master directory table is stored or cached ("cache" is French for hidden) in RAM memory so that when a request for a file stored on the server is made, this table can be accessed and the location of the data found quickly.
3. **Directory hashing:** The master directory table is indexed or "hashed" using a special process that reduces the response time of disk input and output by 30 percent. This index allows the system to find the location of a file by looking at only a few directories.
4. **File caching:** The most heavily used file server files and programs are stored or cached in the server's RAM memory. The first time a file is requested, it is recorded in memory and sorted for future requests. NetWare automatically monitors the area of memory allocated to file caching and decides which files are used more often. Files seldom used are overwritten in memory by new files as requested.
5. **Elevator seeking:** With elevator seeking, the disk read-write head travels across the server hard disk and picks up files in its direction of travel, much like an elevator taking floor requests. When the head reaches the end of the disk, it goes in the other direction, picking up the newly added requests. Picking up requests this way is more efficient than on a first-come, first-served basis, because the read-write head does not have to do as much traveling. Elevator seeking significantly decreases disk wear and tear and increases disk throughput by as much as 50 percent.

NetWare supports most of the popular DOS-based application programs regardless of whether they were designed for a network. Because it doesn't matter if an application was designed to be compatible with NetWare, businesses get the benefits of networking without having to retrain their employees on new application packages. Likewise, businesses don't have to purchase special network versions of the software they already have. (These special network versions do take full advantage of NetWare's features, however, and you should consider special network software when you purchase new programs.)

Another advantage of using a network is that you can control who has access to the network. With NetWare, users are given access to the network on the basis of whether or not they fulfill the access level requirements assigned by the systems administrator. The five access levels are user name, password, trustee, directory, and file attributes. Eight more restrictions can be placed at each level. How to manage this powerful security feature is the focus of this book.

Novell NetWare Version Comparison

Users of NetWare should take time to identify which version of the software they are using. This information is helpful for performing the following tasks:

- Troubleshooting system problems.
- Understanding the capabilities of the system.
- Making upgrading decisions.
- Understanding this book and other informational guides.

A NetWare network differs from version to version in four important areas. The first three have to do with hardware; the last concerns the software that controls user traffic to and from the file server. The four areas are:

1. Workstations, the stand-alone microcomputers connected to the file server.
2. The file server, a microcomputer that is configured to be the network operating system host and may or may not also be a workstation.
3. Cabling and network interface cards (NIC), the special expansion cards that fit inside a microcomputer and connect it to the external cables, thereby making the microcomputer a workstation on the network.
4. The NetWare operating system, the software that coordinates data flow between the file server's hard disk, the printers, the applications and workstation DOS software, and other network resources.

NetWare has a similiar command structure and similar capabilities from version to version. In general, NetWare is divided into three basic versions, 2.0a, 2.1 (includes 2.12), and 2.15. Note that Version 2.15 works like 2.1 but is designed to handle Macintosh hardware. Within each of these three versions—2.0a, 2.1, and 2.15—Novell offers ELS NetWare Level II (ELS II), Advanced NetWare, and NetWare SFT. Versions 2.0a and 2.12 are offered as ELS NetWare Level I (ELS I). A new 32-bit version called NetWare 386 is currently available in one version—3.0 (Version 3.1 will be available first quarter 1990)—and is optimized for a 386-based computer.

This book shows you commands that work with 2.1 and above, currently the most widely used version, and notes any differences unique to 2.0a. Still the administrator should be aware of the subtle differences among versions.

To identify your version, look at your workstation screen when you connect to the server or at the file server : prompt, and type

```
config
```

Make a note of the name and version number that appears. You can make a check by your version number in the list below, where the different versions of NetWare are listed in order of power and functionality.

ELS (Entry Level Solution) Level I

ELS Level II

Advanced NetWare

SFT (System Fault Tolerance) NetWare

NetWare 386

Table 1.1 highlights the features and limitations of the various NetWare versions. You should only concern yourself with the version you have or the next highest version if you are considering an upgrade.

Table 1.1 NetWare Version Features and Limitations

	ELS Level I	ELS Level II	
	below 2.12	below 2.15	2.15
Active users per server	4	8	same
Open concurrent files per server	1024	1024	
Network printers	5	5	
Directory entries/physical drive	24,000	24,000	
Drives per file server	32	32	
Storage capacity in gigabytes (file server)	2GB	2GB	

(continued)

Table 1.1 (continued)

Server RAM	16MB	16MB	
Maximum file size	256MB	256MB	
Dedicated file server	No	No	
Nondedicated file server	Yes	Yes	
Topologies supported	6	12+	
Supports DOS (3.x and up)	Yes	Yes	
Supports NetBIOS applications	No	Yes	
Supports MacIntosh	No	No	Yes
Supports SPX/IPX, OS/2	No	Yes	
Password encryption	No	Yes	same
NetBIOS across bridges	Yes[1]	Yes[1]	
Async Remote Bridge (modem connection to network)	No	Yes	
Resource Accounting	No	Yes[1]	
Enhanced Security	No	Yes[1]	
UPS (Uninterruptable Power Supply) Monitoring	No	No	
Internetworking (two or more networks connected)	No	1 Async Remote	
Add-on LAN Drivers	1	1	

	Advanced NetWare 2.0a	2.1x	2.15
Active users per server	100	100	same
Open concurrent files per server	1024	1024	
Network printers	5	5	
Directory entries/physical drive	24,000	24,000	
Drives per server	32	32	
Storage capacity in gigabytes	2GB	2GB	
Server RAM	16MB	16MB	
Maximum file size	256MB	256MB	
Dedicated file server	Yes	Yes	
Nondedicated file server (optional)	Yes	Yes	
Topologies	12-15	12-15	
Supports DOS (2.x and up)	Yes	Yes	
Supports Macintosh	No	No	Yes
Supports NetBIOS applications, SPX/IPX, OS/2	No	Yes	same
Password encryption	No	Yes	
NetBIOS across bridges	Yes	Yes	
Async Remote Bridge	Yes	Yes	
Resource Accounting	No	Yes	
Enhanced Security	No	Yes	
UPS (Uninterruptable Power Supply) Monitoring	Yes	Yes	
Number of LAN Drivers per server	4	4	
Add-On LAN Drivers	Yes	Yes	
Internetworking	Yes	Yes	

(continued)

Table 1.1 (continued)

	NetWare 386 3.0
Active users per server	250
Open concurrent files per server	100,000
Spooled printers	16
Directory entries/physical drive	
Drives per server	1024
Storage capacity in gigabytes	4
Server RAM	4GB
Maximum file size	4GB
Dedicated file server	Yes
Nondedicated file server	No
Supports DOS (2.x to 4.x)	Yes
Supports Macintosh	No[2]
Supports Named Pipes, NetBIOS, SPX/IPX, OS/2	No[2]
Password encryption	Yes
NetBIOS across bridges	Yes
Async Remote Bridge	Yes (32)
Resource Accounting	Yes
Enhanced Security	Yes
UPS (Uninterruptable Power Supply) Monitoring	Yes

[1]Not included in version 2.0a.
[2]Will be supported in a future version

The first two versions, ELS Level I and ELS Level II, are discussed in the next section. If you are using a higher version, skip ahead to the section that describes your version.

ELS Level I and ELS Level II Versions

The ELS NetWare Level I and Level II are entry-level, cost-effective solutions for networks with a small number of users. Version 2.15 (ELS NetWare Level II only) was designed for use with Apple workstations using the Macintosh Operating System and IBM or compatible hardware. Each system is based on a nondedicated 80286 LAN operating system. *Nondedicated* means that you can use the file server concurrently as a workstation—an important cost-saving feature. With ELS Level I and II, you can have two internal hard disks and five printers—three parallel and two serial. Workstations connected to the server don't require hard disks or floppy drives, a feature to consider when you don't want to spend a lot on workstation hardware. In Table 2.1 you can see the differences between ELS Level I and Level II: number of users, operating systems supported, ability to internetwork and use bridges, resource accounting, password design, as well as other programs.

ELS I handles up to four active users at any one time, and ELS II handles up to eight (although both versions allow virtually an unlimited number of users to be physically connected to the server). It's easy to upgrade ELS NetWare to one of the larger NetWare operating systems, Advanced NetWare or System Fault Tolerant (SFT) NetWare, when the number of users on your network grows.

Advanced NetWare Version 2.0a

Advanced NetWare Version 2.0a is the oldest version of Novell NetWare and is no longer available. However, we have included this section since there are users who own this version and may not have upgraded to other versions. It catered to the larger business environment by allowing more users to be on the system. It was the first version to give you the option of deciding whether the file server is dedicated or nondedicated—so you can choose whether to make your file server a workstation as well. Version 2.0a works only with DOS 2.x and above. Commands and functions are identical to those of ELS version 2.Oa, but you also get a built-in electronic mail program called E-Mail, which is described below.

Version 2.0a's E-Mail program lets you compose, send, and file network mail consisting of documents, letters, files, and memos. Network mail can be sent to users or groups or stored until a user accesses it. The Express Mail feature notifies users when a message is waiting.

Advanced NetWare Version 2.1x

Advanced NetWare Version 2.1x brings the features of a powerful minicomputer system to the network. This version, with more than 100 enhancements over version 2.0a, is a significant improvement over the previous version. Its menu-driven utilities such as PRINTDEF, PCONSOLE, and an enhanced version of SYSCON make network management simpler. The systems administrator can add or delete users in bulk, thanks to the new MAKEUSER utility. The Virtual Console feature, or FCONSOLE, allows the system administrator to manage the network from any workstation on the internet. SYSCON is an accounting and billing feature with which you can charge users for the time they spend on the network. Because users are restricted to a specific workstation, directory, or time period, network security is increased. Password encryption, intruder detection, and allowable log-ins have also been added. All these features make Version 2.1x a more productive, efficient, and secure operating system.

Advanced NetWare Version 2.15

Version 2.15 was designed to support the Macintosh Operating System on either IBM compatible or on Apple Macintosh hardware. With this version you get all the benefits of NetWare without losing the easy-to-use features of the Macintosh environment. The command utilities and menus are identicial to those of the other Advanced NetWare versions.

SFT NetWare

SFT NetWare (System Fault Tolerance) with its two levels of data security, decreases the chance of data loss on your network. On the first level is a function called Hot Fix (included in 2.0a SFT Level I and 2.1x) that prevents data loss in the following ways:

- By provides consistent directory structures.
- By requires the system to verify the directory structure when you power up.
- By provides disk read-after-write verification and defective block flagging.

The second level (included in 2.0a SFT Level II and 2.1x) provides you with *disk mirroring, disk duplexing,* and *transaction tracking*, all of which are discussed below.

1. With *disk mirroring,* SFT duplicates your entire primary disk on a second hard disk. If your original disk fails, the duplicate, or *mirrored,* disk takes over automatically. This keeps you from losing your important data.
2. With *disk duplexing,* SFT can duplicate the entire disk system. This means that the cable unit, drive controllers, or power supply can be duplicated as well as the hard disk. Disk duplexing prevents data from being lost should any component fail in the channel from the server to the disk.
3. With the *Transaction Tracking System (TTS)* offered by SFT, you can preserve the integrity of your database in the event that an application, a workstation, or the file server crashes before a transaction is completed. Chiefly this program protects information from being corrupted or destroyed if a failure occurs during a database update. It does this by treating database changes as a single unit of work (a transaction) to be either wholly completed or wholly abandoned. In case of a failure, the transaction is wholly abandoned and TTS rolls back database changes to the previous complete transaction written to the disk and verifed.

All fault-tolerant features in SFT work automatically; however, you can select whether to enable them when you install the operating system. Moreover, users won't notice them, so the work that SFT does will not interrupt the normal operation of the network or workstation.

NetWare 386

This latest version of NetWare has been shipped as of August, 1989. It was developed to take advantage of the model 386 file server. A major improvement is the new design that takes advantage of the 80386 and 80486 microprocessors. One new feature is a built-in print server utility that will allow users to access up to 16 network printers. It will also increase the possible number of active users from 100 to 250. Enhanced features that increase reliability such as Hot Fix, Transaction Tracking, and disk mirroring and duplexing have been included. Security is increased through the creation of a *security shield* that better protects data such as passwords and resources such as the file server.

It is upward compatible with previous versions of NetWare installed on a 386 file server. Since the product is also going to be available in a version 3.1 in early 1990, other features may not be finalized. Check with Novell if you are considering a 386 version of NetWare for more details.

The Duties of an Administrator Versus Those of a Systems Consultant

The systems administrator must know what tasks are his or hers to perform, and so must the consultant. The tasks involved with running a network can be divided into two categories: those performed by the systems administrator and those performed by a systems consultant or in-house systems specialist. The duties of the consultant are described below, and those of the systems administrator are described in the next section.

The Systems Specialist's Responsibilities

Each Novell NetWare network should have been installed by a person authorized to do the job. Usually this person is the one who sold the system; in a larger company this person would likely be a systems specialist. Novell requires its resellers to complete a five-day training course at an authorized training center and have a file server installed in their office. If you purchased your system from a reseller, he or she should either be able to perform most of the duties in Table 1.2 or be able to recommend someone who can perform them. If you are searching for a reseller, systems consultant, or hiring an in-house specialist to perform these duties, make sure you obtain a list of references from that person.

Table 1.2 Systems Specialist Duties

1. Identify hardware and software needs based on the number of users on the network and how fast the network will grow.
2. Recommend proper topology based on the desired speed of the network, how fast it will grow, the input and output rate to the server, and the number of shared applications on the network.
3. Acquire or recommend software and hardware based on:
   - The compatibility of applications software in the network.
   - The model and the microprocessor speed of the server and workstations.
   - Budgeted cost.
   - Applications hardware requirements.
   - The compatibility of existing equipment.
   - System backup medium (tape drive).
   - Backup power supply.
4. Design and lay out the system configuration based on:
   - The position of the file server, workstations, printers, backup devices and backup power supply.
   - The type of cabling and network interface cards (NICs).
   - The bridge software to connect: one type of topology to another, one server to another, or a remote workstation to a local workstation by way of a modem.
   - The gateway hardware to connect: workstation(s) to a minicomputer, or workstation(s) to mainframe.
5. Install and test network hardware, including these items:
   - Cable connectors and intercabling devices to workstations.
   - Server and workstation cards.
   - Server or workstation memory.
   - Printer connections to the server or servers .
   - Gateway hardware.
   - Peripherals such as monitors, drives, and modems.
   - Backup medium type and power supply.
6. Install and test the network software by:
   - Preparing server disk drives and memory.
   - Generating the Novell operating system.
   - Preparing workstation boot disks.
   - Loading other network utilities such as the Network Assistant and Keeptrack (these are discussed in Part I of this book).
   - Installing and configuring electronic mail and communications software.
   - Configuring and testing bridge software.
7. Fine tune the performance of the network by:
   - Running benchmark tests of speed and usage loads.
   - Using utility programs that test performance.
8. Install, configure and load applications software on the server and/or the workstations.
9. Create menus and login scripts to interface with less experienced users that:
   - Start applications.
   - Provide a turnkey system based on the type of business or user needs.
10. Train the systems administrator and users to perform network related tasks such as:
    - Starting up and powering down the network.

    Logging in and out of the system.

- Printing on the network.
- Sending electronic mail messages

11. Provide ongoing maintenance and hardware or software upgrades to:
    - The NetWare and operating system.
    - The applications software.
    - The memory for the servers or workstations.
    - New hard drives or additional storage devices that work with servers.
    - New servers and workstations.
    - The network backup system.

The Systems Administrator's Responsibilities

Some systems administrators have achieved a very sophisticated technical level and can perform some of the systems specialist duties listed in Table 1.2. However, the duties they are expected to perform are listed in Table 1.3.

Table 1.3 The Systems Administrator's Duties

1. Documenting the system in an organized, up-to-date format.
2. Creating and maintaining efficient file server structure.
3. Backing up the system.
4. Adding and deleting users.
5. Assigning security and trustee rights.
6. Maintaining ongoing user support.
7. Troubleshooting and monitoring system performance.
8. Accounting for user time, date and workstation resources.
9. Managing network and local printer print jobs.
10. Changing passwords.
11. Mapping logical and search drives.
12. Measuring server disk space.
13. Managing directory structure.
14. Supporting electronic mail products.
15. Installing and loading applications software.
16. Installing new or moving workstations.
17. Designing the menus.
18. Sending messages.

The tasks listed in Table 1.3 are discussed in Chapter 4. Adding new workstations is discussed in Chapter 5. When you add a workstation for the first time, do it under the supervision of your systems specialist.

Network-wide user support depends on the systems administrator. You must have the information and skills to handle problems when they arise and answer questions from the users. To obtain this level of expertise, study your network carefully. Once you have learned about its features and structure, troubleshooting won't take as much time and you'll be able to concentrate on increasing the performance of your system.

You will begin the hands-on exploration of your system in the next part of this book. We will use a model system as an example of how to walk through your Novell NetWare Network. You will also learn to document valuable information about your system so that later you can become a master at running your network.

Chapter 2

A Hands-on Tutorial

The first step in working with a network is to get comfortable with handling its resources in a hands-on style. If you were working with a new software program, such as a word processor, you would most likely try a typical task to perform such as creating and printing a letter. A new spreadsheet program might inspire you to try your own budget. To learn the basics of a database program, you could tackle your department's phone directory. With a network, it is not so easy to think of what task to practice in order to learn about the network. The purpose of this section is to give you a structured path to follow, allowing you to learn about your network resources. You will identify parts of your network using an exploratory hands-on tutorial featuring the CONFIG, NVER, SYSCON, SESSION, and FILER commands.

In addition to practicing these commands, you will learn to document the important features and settings in your system for future reference. Each exercise refers you to a form and instructions on how to organize this information into a system notebook. Appendix B shows a recommended table of contents for such a notebook. This section will show you how to document the following:

- File server location and name.
- Network topology.
- Each file server.
- Each printer.
- Each workstation.
- System login script.
- Group names, user lists, and rights.
- User names, login scripts and rights.
- Custom designed user menus.

Once you understand this information, you will be able to manage your network better. Troubleshooting problems or making changes will be easier and take less time. You will develop a confidence about your resources and make more informed decisions. The next section discusses the first step of your management task: identifying file servers and topology.

Identifying and Documenting Servers and Topology

Whether you need to troubleshoot problems or plan to expand on the network, knowing the location, number of file servers, and type of topology is important. The first question a good technical support person will ask is what version of NetWare and what type of connection hardware you are using . Since the components that make up the connection hardware are often cables and cards that are not visible, it is much easier to look for this information on the file server using NetWare commands.

Let's take a look at the location and number of file servers on your system. Your systems specialist should have the location of the file server(s). If they are in another building or site, make a note of it. Once you have located each file server, you should document the following information using the format shown in Table 2.1.

Table 2.1 File Server Inventory

File Server Purpose	NetWare Name	Location	Model
Accounting	ACCY	Office 29	Compaq 286
Marketing	MRKTG	Office 30	Compaq 386

You will find a form for this information in Appendix B. Take a few moments to fill it out now as the first step to documenting your Novell network.

Next you will discover the type of network interface card and topology used by your network. At the file server monitor screen at the (:) prompt type

```
config [Enter]
```

This will give you the information shown in Figure 2.1.

```
Number of service Processes: [ ]

LAN A Configuration information:
   Network Address: [              ] [              ]
   Hardware   Type: [              ]
   Hardware Setting: IRQ = [    ]  I/O Base = [    ]
   RAM Buffer at [              ]
```

Figure 2.1 Hardware configuration information for the file server.

This information should be written down on your file server worksheet as using this form which can be found in Appendix B.

The information that appears in the [ ] (brackets) after **Hardware Type:** tells you what type of network interface card your system is using and the topology used. Using Table 2.2 as a reference, note your system's topology next to the type in this form (found in Appendix B).

Table 2.2 Network Interface Cards and Related Topology

Network Interface Card	Topology
• Rx-Net, Standard Microsystems ARCNET, Pure Data ARCNET	Distributed Star
• Ethernet, 3-COM, G-Net Gateway	Linear Bus
• S-Net Novell	Star
• Proteon, IBM TRN/A, IBM PC Adaptor	Token-passing or star-wired ring

Topology layouts look like Figure 2.2. Knowing the type of topology your network uses is useful in understanding expansion needs and other hardware devices used to connect the workstations to the file server.

Logging in as SUPERVISOR

The code word SUPERVISOR used as a login name gives you all rights to network resources. Its power should be well understood before using any of the network menu utilities. Although this exploration through the network does *not* alter any of the security settings and you can proceed with confidence:, you may want to review the supervisor functions using your course notes or the Novell Supervisor's Guide. To log into your network now and begin the SYSCON portion of the exploration tutorial, at the login prompt type:

SUPERVISOR[Enter]
password[Enter] (see your systems consultant if you do not know it or call Novell)

You should see various drive mappings appear on screen (if MAP DISPLAY is ON, see "Mapping" to control this setting) and an F> prompt your drive letter may differ; if it is not a drive letter F through Z, type F:[Enter]). You are now ready to use the SYSCON menu.

Bringing Up the SYSCON Menu

This menu utility gives you, the system administrator, the greatest power and flexibility in controlling users, network security and access to application programs. It also provides you access to submenus that will help you troubleshoot and improve the performance of your network. Let's go through the different choices under the SYSCON menu. You should have logged into the network using **supervisor** as the login name and you now have an F> prompt on the screen.

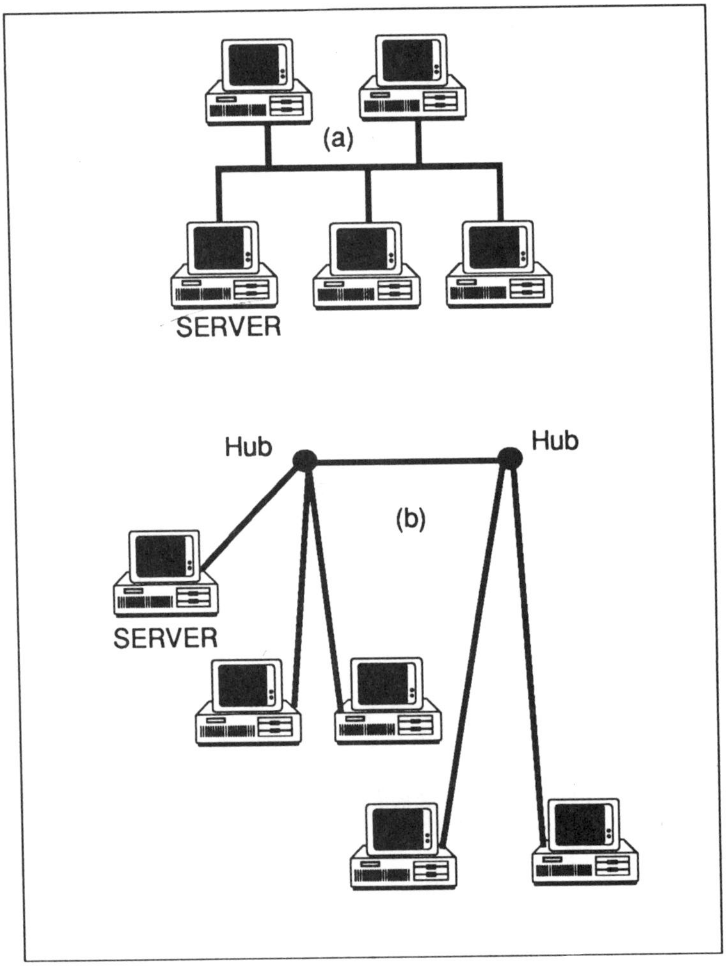

Figure 2.2 (a) Linear bus, (b) distributed star.

TYPE/PRESS	RESULT:
SYSCON [Enter]	Displays the SYSCON menu

For 2.1 and above your screen appears as in Figure 2.3.

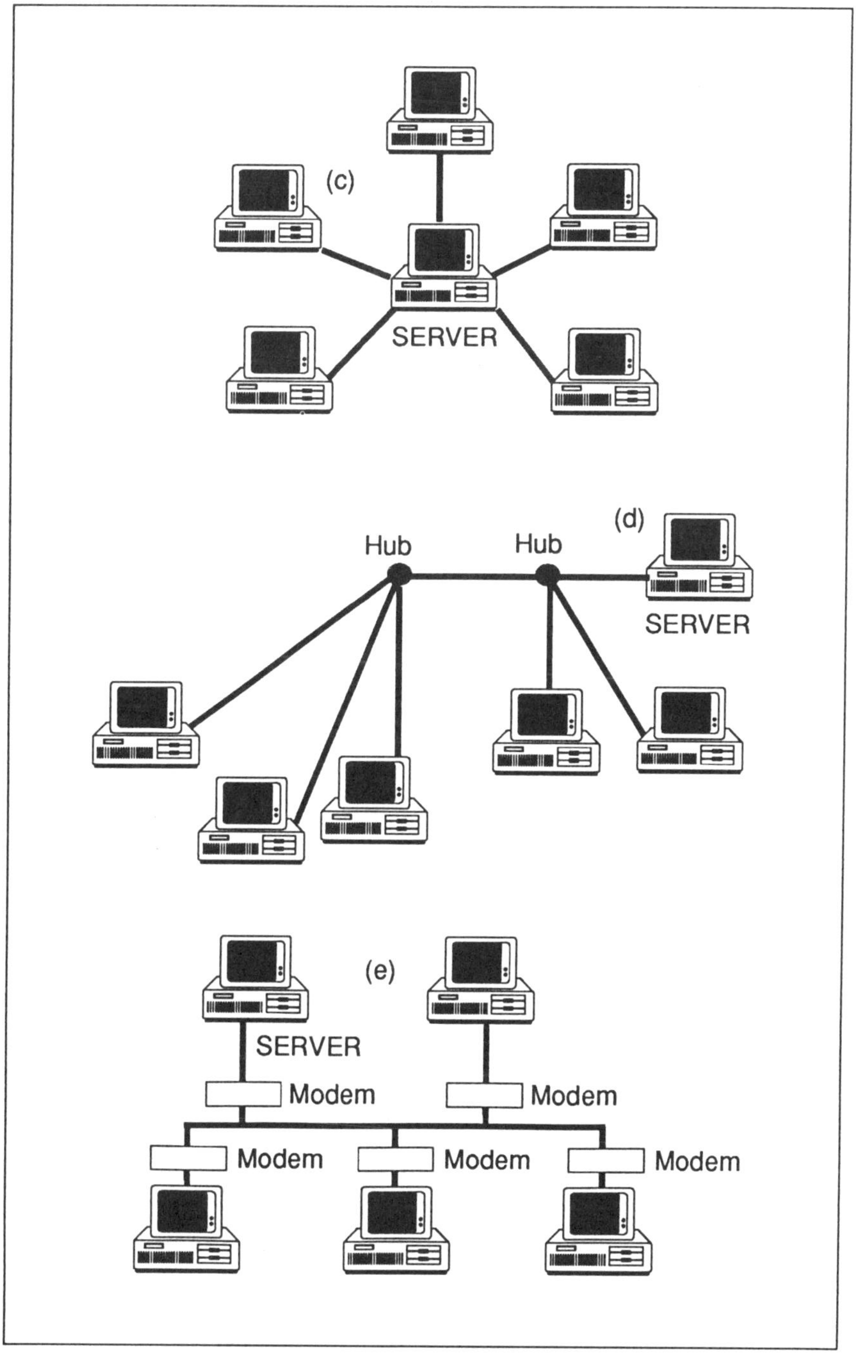

Figure 2.2 (c) star, (d) token-passing ring, and (e) broad band basic topology layouts.

The SYSCON menu offers the following menu choices:

- Change CurrentServer
- File Server Information
- Group Information
- User Information
- System login script (2.0a) Supervisor's options (2.1)

You will now learn to access each file server and document important information about it.

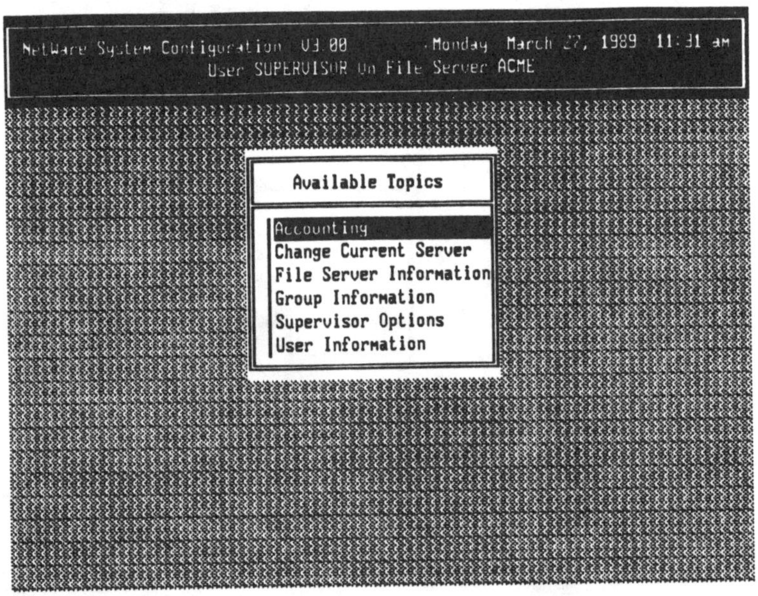

Figure 2.3 Version 2.1 and above SYSCON main menu.

Listing File Servers

The file server is the most important resource for storing data on the network. Your system contains at least one file server. To list the file servers on your system, using SYSCON:

TYPE/PRESS	RESULT:
SYSCON [Enter]	Displays SYSCON main menu
F [Enter]	Selects File Server Information and displays list of file servers

Esc	Exits Known NetWare Servers menu
Esc	Exits SYSCON
Y [Enter]	Confirms Exit

The Known NetWare Servers list is displayed as in Figure 2.4.

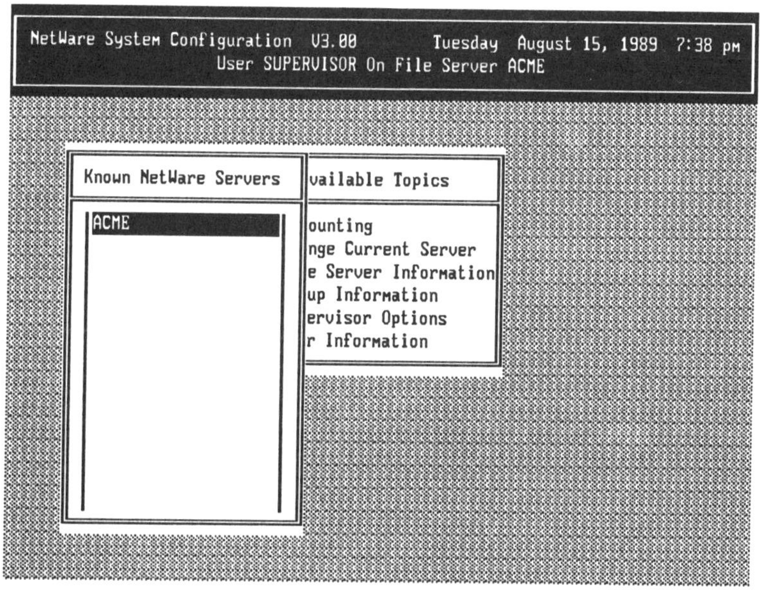

Figure 2.4 Known NetWare file servers.

Note that our example uses a file server named ACME. ACME's design is used throughout this book to show how a typical network looks. You should be able to document the same information we present about ACME for your own network.

This menu is also used to find out information on each file server, such as names, NetWare version, workstation and node address, number of workstations in use, and volumes supported as shown in Figure 2.5.

To find our this information at a workstation connected to the file server using SYSCON:

TYPE/PRESS	RESULT:
SYSCON [Enter]	Displays SYSCON main menu
F [Enter]	Selects and displays File Server Information
select any file server name [Enter]	Displays the selected file server's information
Esc	Returns you to file server list
Esc	Returns you to SYSCON main menu
Esc	Exits SYSCON
Y [Enter]	Confirms Exit

Print the server information screen to document your server name, NetWare version, and other information shown in Figure 2.5. Repeat this step for any additional file servers on your system.

You are now ready to document and identify your system's printers.

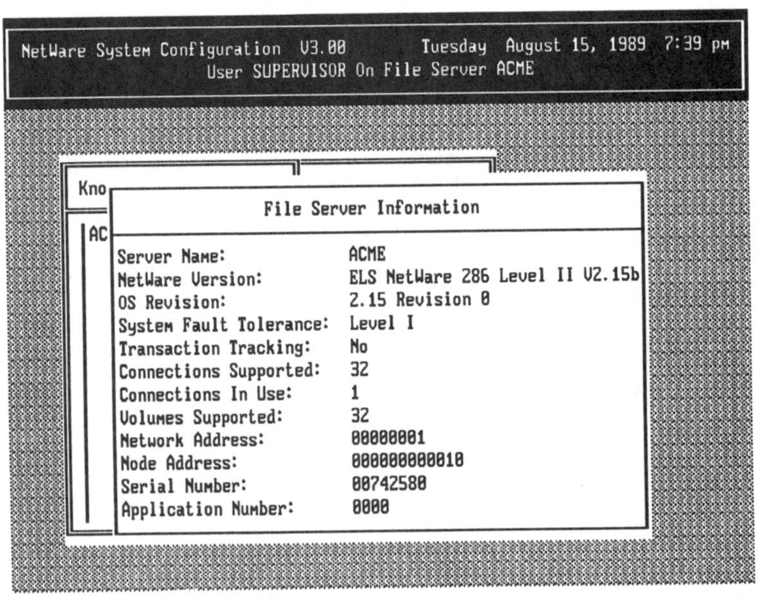

Figure 2.5 File Server Information.

Identifying and Documenting Printers

To identify the printers on each file server, you should first determine your system's printer configuration. There are two methods to configure and access network printers using NetWare:

1. Connect printers to a file server; access them using printer numbers 0 to 4 or 6 (depends on the number of printers supported by your version of NetWare; see the Introduction to this book).
2. Connect printers to a workstation and create a special device called a *print server* that allows users network printer access in addition to a file server's printers. Current versions of NetWare do not include a built-in function that creates a print server, it must be created using a third-party utility program. Part II of this book describes such programs in the section "Printer Configuration."

To determine how many printers are attached to a file server using the console command P at the file server (console) keyboard:

TYPE/PRESS	RESULT:
P [Enter]	Displays the configuration of network printers attached to the file server

To determine how many printers are attached to a file server Version 2.0a using the QUEUE menu:

TYPE/PRESS	RESULT:
QUEUE [Enter]	Displays the QUEUE menu
S [Enter]	Selects Select Printer option

To determine the number of printers attached to a print server, identify each print server using the 2.1 and above PCONSOLE menu at a workstation connected to the file server:

TYPE/PRESS	RESULT:
PCONSOLE [Enter]	Displays the PCONSOLE main menu
Print S [Enter]	Selects Print Server Information
select any print server name [Enter]	Displays information about the print server

Once you have identified your network's printers, create a diagram documenting their location—either a file server or print server (make sure to include the name of the file or print server) similar to Table 2.3.

Table 2.3 Network Printer Configuration

Printer Model/Name	Location	Port/Number
HP Laserjet II	ACME file server	LPT1/0
NEC P7	ACME file server	LPT2/1
Epson FX-286	ACME file server	LPT3/2
HP Laserjet II	ACME file server	COM1/3
Apple Laserwriter	ACME file server	COM2/4
HP Laserjet II	ITD-18 print server	LPT1/1
Epson FX-286	ACME file server	LPT2/5

Identifying and Documenting Workstations

As the systems supervisor, you are responsible for troubleshooting and supporting the entire system. It is a good practice to keep a well-organized and up-to-date record of the various workstations in your environment. Record repairs, document a problem history, write down serial numbers, and keep a vendor support telephone list with hours of operation, if possible. This makes troubleshooting and planning easier and office-to-office moves smoother. When a user's needs change and thus require different hardware or software, workstation components can be exchanged or upgraded accordingly. Inventory is also more easily controlled when a record of each computer can be produced.

The first step in taking an inventory as systems administrator is to identify which microcomputers are configured as network workstations. You can do this several ways: by checking for a cable running from the computer to the file server, other workstation, or active hub or wire center (since cable can be hidden under floors or inside walls, this method is difficult); booting the workstation with a diskette that attaches the computer to the network; or asking your systems consultant to physically walk you through the network.

The next step is to mark each workstation with an *identifier*, or label, that tells you its model or make and a digit (in case of duplicate models). For example, PC-001 would tell you that the computer is a microcomputer similar to an IBM PC, AT-001 describes an IBM AT, and COMPAQ 286-001 signifies a COMPAQ 286 Deskpro. If the workstation's NIC (Network Interface Card) has an address setting, include it also. You might even label the department or user name in addition, in case you need to move or repair the equipment. Attach the label to the computer so it is visible. Later, if you need to repair or move the workstation, you will be able to locate it easily. Once labeled, record the list of identifiers on paper as shown in Figure 2.6.

Efficient network planning and expansion depends on knowing about current resources. For example, when you decide to add a workstation using an ARCNET, G-Net, IBM Token-Passing Ring, or TBR Proteon network interface card, you will need to set a series of switches unique from those already installed in the network. These are often referred to as the *station address* of the card and should be marked on the backplate of the card, which is located in a slot on the back of the workstation. The setting of these switches is discussed in Chapter 5 of this book.

This documentation keeps you from having to open the back of each workstation when you add a new one, just to assure that the number you have set is unique.

After NetWare has seen this station address or has made the connection to the actual workstation, it assigns a special internal address to the workstation on the server known as the *physical station address*. To find this address:

Workstation Identifier Master Listing
Company ________
As of ___/___/___

Identifier	Station Address	Physical Address	Serial No	Location/User Name
AF-1	33	1F	123456789	ACCOUNTING-MARY
PC-1	255	FF	987654321	EXECUTIVE-TOM
XT-1	254	FE	135792468	ANALYST-PAT

Figure 2.6 Workstation identifiers.

- Boot the workstation(s).
- Log into the network using any user name.

TYPE/PRESS	**RESULT:**
SESSION [Enter]	Displays SESSION main menu
U [Enter]	Selects User List
name of user (Supervisor) [Enter]	Selects Current User
D [Enter]	Selects Display User Info

Your screen should look like Figure 2.7.

The last two numbers or character combination of the Network Node display is the physical address. This address only changes if you replace the network card with another or change station address switches. Some functions such as setting workstation restrictions for a user require that you supply this number when installing it.

The next step is to determine the *configuration*, or type, of equipment and software installed in each workstation. This information represents several variables that could ease

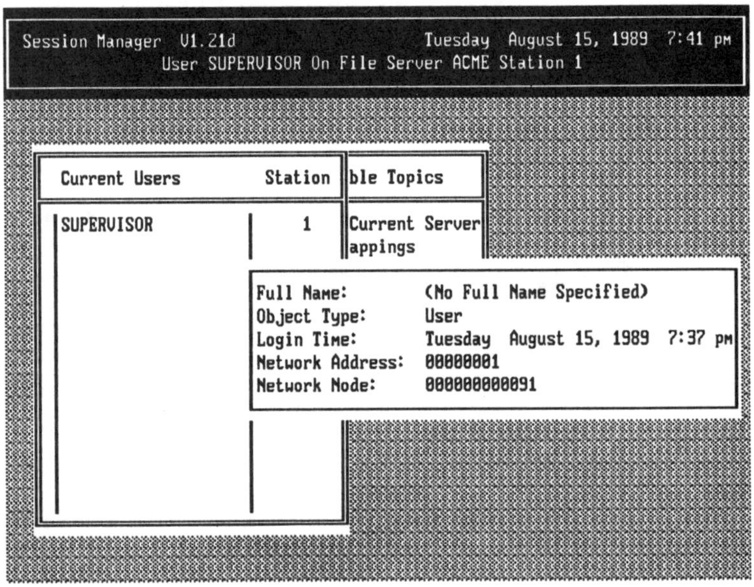

Figure 2.7 User Info Screen.

the problem-solving process. Hardware factors such as memory, hard disk space, output ports, and display adaptors are common causes of workstation failure. Software factors such as operating system version, CONFIG.SYS parameters, and location of applications program files can also lead to problems. For example, if you add a memory adaptor to a workstation, the CONFIG.SYS file is usually edited to include the device driver file to make the computer recognize the new memory. Since hardware problems are too often assumed to be network-related, making a note of special lines in the CONFIG.SYS file will be useful.

Files that are used in the NetWare shell to connect the workstation to the network are also worth noting. They are either the IPX.COM and ANET.COM, NET2.COM,

NET3.COM, or NET4.COM, depending on which version of NetWare you are using. NETBIOS.EXE and INT2F.COM may also be found on workstations used to run an application requiring NetBIOS.

Some older applications such as NetRemote that provided peer-to-peer communications used NetBIOS, but few others, if any, continue to use it. Each hard disk computer must contain these on the disk; floppy drive workstations store the files on a special boot diskette. These files should have been created by your systems consultant and stored on a diskette in the systems administrator's information binder as well as documented for each workstation containing them.

If you take the time to outline these specifications now, you will be better equipped to manage the crisis situation. Table 2.4 is an example of a chart used to document and identify your network workstations.

Tip: To check a computer's total conventional (up to 640K) RAM memory quickly, use the DOS CHKDSK command.

Table 2.4 Workstation Inventory

XYZ Company Workstation Inventory as of: 1/1/90

Identifier tag—type/number	PC-001	AT-001
Station Address (Arcnet)	243	247
Physical Address (via SESSION)	F3	F7
Serial Number	1423445	1423567
Location/User	Reception	Accounting
User Name	Angie	Mark
Hardware related:		
Manufacturer	IBM	IBM
Hard disk size	none	20MB
Free space		10.5MB
Manufacturer		Seagate
Conventional RAM memory	640K	640K
Add-on memory	none	2MB
Clock/Calendar	yes	yes
Display type	Mono IBM	EGA IBM
Printer (local)	none	Epson FX
Ports—parallel	LPT1	LPT1, 2
—serial	COM1	COM1, 2
Modem type/speed	none	Hayes 1200
Internal/External		internal
COM1 or COM2 port		COM1
Keyboard type	std	enhanced
Floppy disk drives	2-360K	1-360K 1-1.2MB
Software related:		
Network boot disk operating system/version		

	DOS 3.1	DOS 3.2
Shell files	ANET, IPX	ANET, IPX
CONFIG.SYS special parameters	none	video driver
AUTOEXEC.BAT	prompt, shell	prompt, path, shell
Directory/name/serial number stand-alone software on local hard disk		
Word processing	none	WordPerfect 5.0 WP50 12345xv
Spreadsheet	1-2-3 2.0 123-45678	1-2-3 3.0 123r3 123-98765
Database	none	dBASE III + db3 345-yt890
Communications	none	Smartcom sc 34567-9887
Graphics		Harvard Graphics hg 345987-90
Other		IBM 36 emulation

Documenting a File Server Hard Disk

It is good management practice to keep track of what is stored on the file server hard disk. You can do this easily using the FILER menu utility to document your current subdirectory structure. Your file server will contain four special directories created and required by NetWare:

1. LOGIN: Stores LOGIN.EXE and SLIST.EXE commands.
2. PUBLIC: Stores all command-line utility files accessable to users.
3. MAIL: Creates a subdirectory for each user under a user ID number; stores login scripts and mail items if they exist.
4. SYSTEM: Stores NET$OS.EXE and other security-related system files known as *bindary* files, or files that bind or hold the network together.

The files in these directories should not be changed, deleted, or otherwise tampered with.

The first step to documenting your system's unique design is to establish a listing of subdirectory names as shown in Figure 2.8.

To do this using the FILER menu, log in at a workstation as supervisor, change the directory to the root using CD\, and at the DOS prompt type:

TYPE/PRESS	RESULT:
FILER [Enter]	Displays the FILER main menu
SU [Enter]	Selects Subdirectory Information

A list of subdirectories will appear. Move the cursor to each one and make a note of each name using the form provided in Appendix B. Note that each subdirectory's structure is documented using the format in Appendix B.

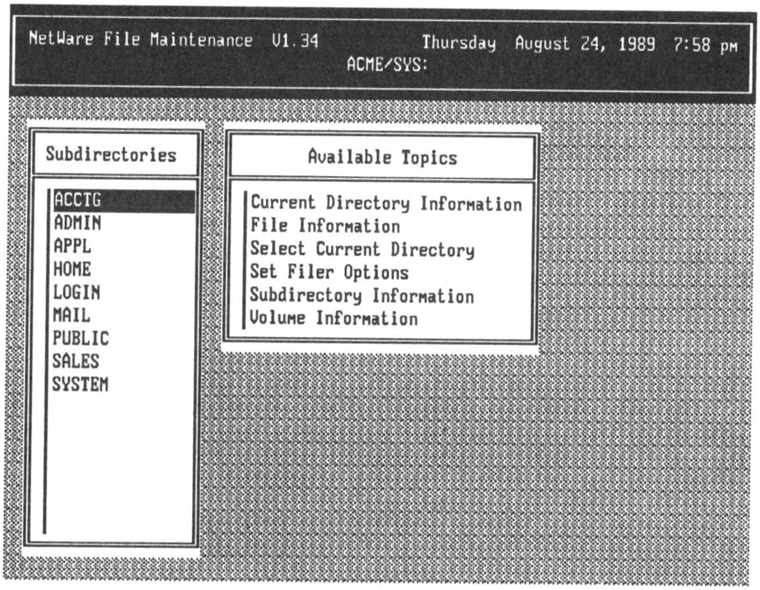

Figure 2.8A

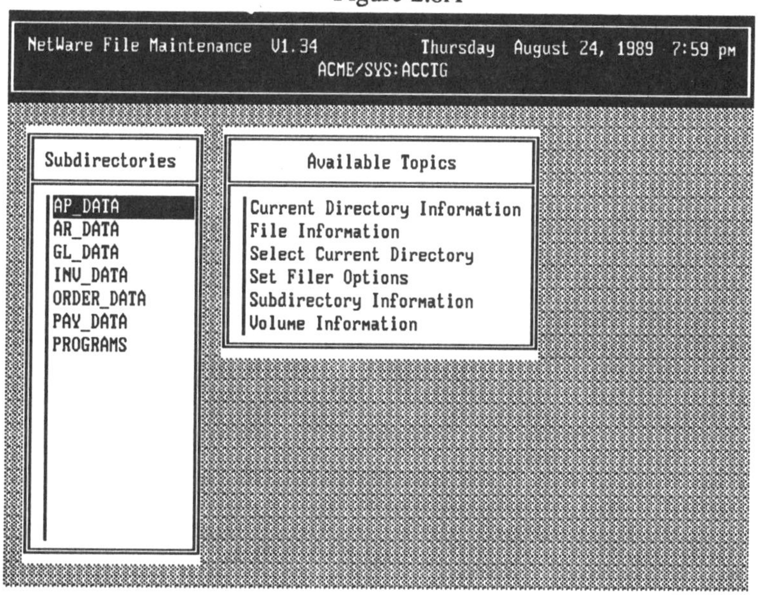

Figure 2.8 (A–G) Subdirectory names of ACME file server.

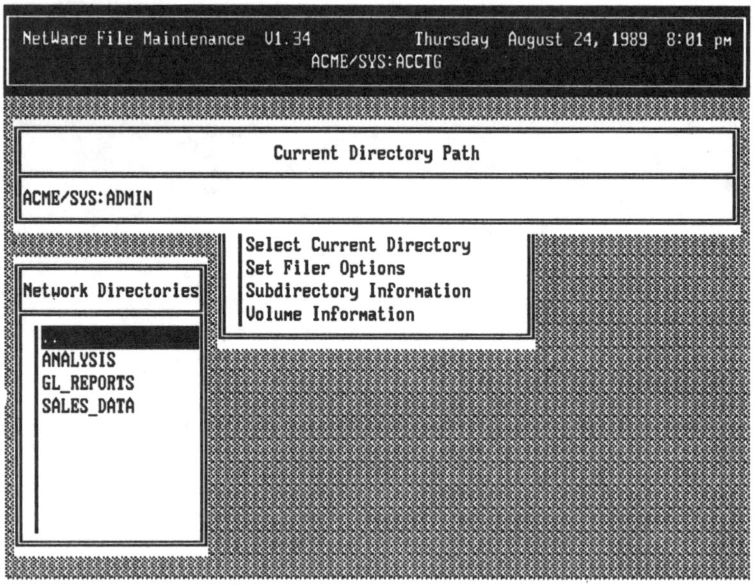

Figure 2.8C

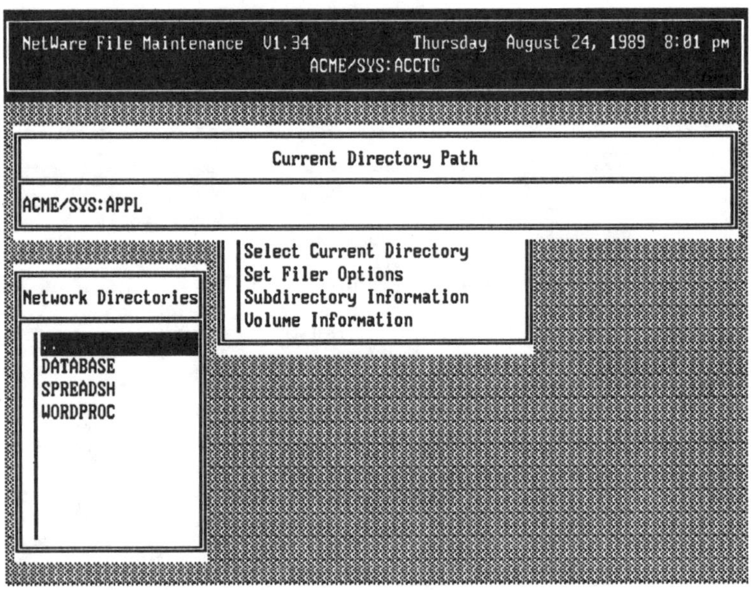

Figure 2.8D

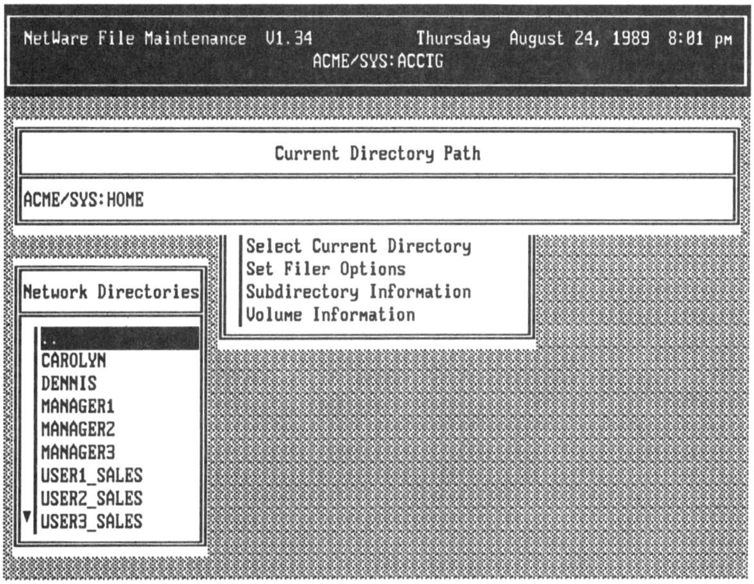

Figure 2.8E

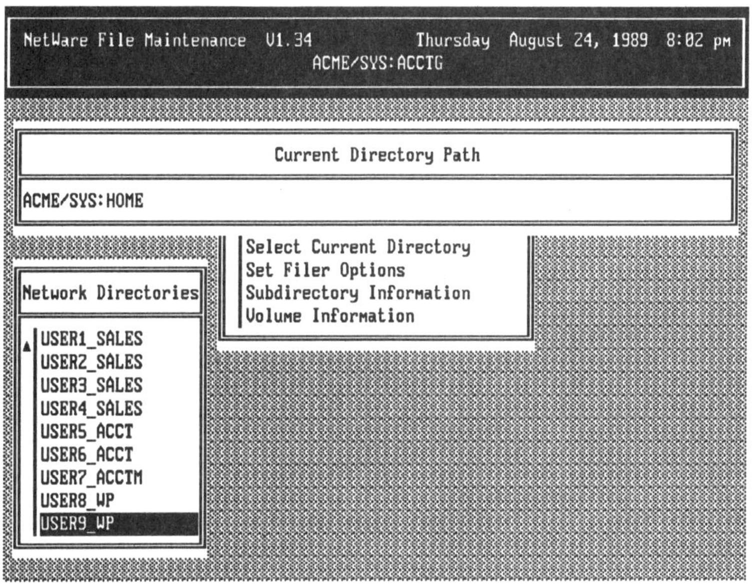

Figure 2.8F

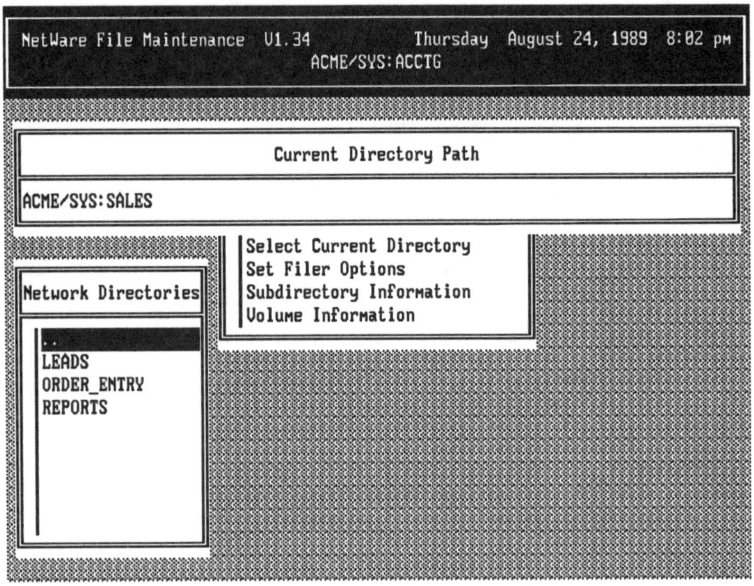

Figure 2.8G

Esc	Returns to FILER main menu
S [Enter]	Selects Current Directory
select any directory name [Enter]	Displays its subdirectories

You should create a directory structure reference card as shown in Appendix B. It is a good idea to also document what is stored in each directory. For example, in the Acme file server, each subdirectory has been documented with a brief description about the contents, users who have access, and other information regarding read/write issues in Table 2.5.

Table 2.5 Acme File Server Hard Disk Documentation

ACME/SYS:ACCTG: Contains a directory for each type of accounting data file and one for the accounting software program.
User access: Group ACCTG, users DENNIS and CAROLYN.

ACME/SYS:ADMIN: Contains administrative data files such as word processed documents used for analysis, mailing list database, and general ledger reports updated by administrative users.

User access: MANAGER 1, MANAGER 2, MANAGER 3, and users DENNIS and CAROLYN.

ACME/SYS:APPL: Contains all applications programs—word processing in \WORDPROC, spreadsheet in \SPREADSH, and database in \DATABASE.

User access: Users have read, open, and search access only.

ACME/SYS:HOME: Contains a private directory for each user named identical to user login ID.

User access: Each user has all rights to his/her directory only.

ACME/SYS:SALES: Contains sales data files such as monthly sales leads, orders, and quotes. Graphs and spreadsheet forecast reports are also included.

User access: Group SALES, accounting manager (MANAGER 1), and admin manager (MANAGER 2).

Note that the directory name includes the file server name, volume and full path. For example, the directory name

ACME/SYS:APPL/WP

represents the file server ACME, volume SYS, subdirectory APPL \WP. Note that NetWare accepts a / (slash) or \ (backslash) to separate the file server name from the volume and each subdirectory from the next. DOS uses the \(backslash) only to separate subdirectory names. In addition, the : (colon) is used in NetWare to separate the volume name from the first subdirectory. Now that you have identified your file server directory structure, you can use SYSCON to view which users have access to each directory.

Exploring the System Login Script

A system login script is a special optional NetWare file with stored commands that allow a uniform, custom entry into the network for all users when executed. It can be designed to automatically assign logical and search drive mappings for all or individual users upon login, run external applications programs or DOS commands for all or individual users, display a custom system menu or message, or control program controls with logical IF statements. When users require unique commands upon login, it is best to create an individual login script rather than trying to customize the system login for that user or user group. Individual logins should also be documented as shown later in this section. Designing login scripts are discussed in detail in the section "Logging Into the Network" in Chapter 4.

The objective of this task is to be able to document and identify commands executed by the system at login for all users and therefore help them avoid issuing redundant commands. Figure 2.9 shows an example of our model system's login script.

```
NetWare System Configuration  V3.00      Saturday  August 19, 1989  11:38 am
                        User DENNIS On File Server ACME

                              System Login Script

MAP DISPLAY OFF
MAP ERRORS OFF
WRITE "Logging onto Acme Fireworks Company Network  . . We guarantee you a
BANGUP TIME!"
PAUSE
FIRE PHASERS 5 TIMES
WRITE "Good ";GREETING_TIME; " ";LOGIN_NAME
WRITE "\r\n"
IF DAY_OF_WEEK="MONDAY" THEN WRITE "OGIM! Here we go again... another week
another million dollars !"
IF DAY_OF_WEEK="WEDNESDAY" THEN WRITE "It's Hump Day.  Everything is downhill
from here!"
IF HOUR24 <= "15" AND DAY_OF_WEEK="FRIDAY" THEN WRITE "TGIF! The weekend
countdown has begun."
IF DAY_OF_WEEK="SATURDAY" THEN WRITE "Have a WONDERFUL WEEKEND!"
```

Figure 2.9A Model system login script.

```
NetWare System Configuration  V3.00      Saturday  August 19, 1989  11:40 am
                        User DENNIS On File Server ACME

                              System Login Script

countdown has begun."
IF DAY_OF_WEEK="SATURDAY" THEN WRITE "Have a WONDERFUL WEEKEND!"
IF LOGIN_NAME = "SUPERVISOR" THEN BEGIN
MAP S4:=SYS:SYSTEM
END
IF MEMBER OF "ADMIN" THEN BEGIN
MAP M:=SYS:ACCTG\GL_DATA
END
IF MEMBER OF "SALES" THEN BEGIN
MAP S:=SYS:ACCTG\ORDER_DATA
END
IF MEMBER OF "ACCTG" THEN BEGIN
MAP M:=SYS:ACCTG\GL_DATA; N:=SYS:ACCTG\AR_DATA; O:=SYS:ACCTG\AP_DATA;
P:=SYS:ACCTG\PAY_DATA; Q:=SYS:ACCTG\INV_DATA; S:=SYS:ACCTG\ORDER_DATA
END
MAP F:=SYS:
MAP G:=SYS:HOME\%LOGIN_NAME
```

Figure 2.9B

```
NetWare System Configuration  V3.00        Saturday  August 19, 1989  11:40 am
                        User DENNIS On File Server ACME

                               System Login Script

MAP M:=SYS:ACCTG\GL_DATA; N:=SYS:ACCTG\AR_DATA; O:=SYS:ACCTG\AP_DATA;
P:=SYS:ACCTG\PAY_DATA; Q:=SYS:ACCTG\INV_DATA; S:=SYS:ACCTG\ORDER_DATA
END
MAP F:=SYS:
MAP G:=SYS:HOME\%LOGIN_NAME
MAP H:=SYS:APPL\SPREADSH; I:=SYS:SALES; J:=SYS:APPL\WORDPROC
MAP K:=SYS:APPL\DATABASE; L:=SYS:APPL\SPREADSHEET; R:=SYS:ADMIN
MAP S1:=SYS:PUBLIC
MAP S2:=SYS:PUBLIC\%MACHINE\%OS\%OS_VERSION
MAP S3:=SYS:ACCTG\PROGRAMS
SET PROMPT="$P$G"
DOS VERIFY ON
DOS BREAK ON
COMSPEC=S2:COMMAND.COM
DRIVE G:
#CAPTURE P0 NB NFF TI5
EXIT "MENU ACME"
```

Figure 2.9C

Notice that the first two commands, MAP DISPLAY OFF and MAP ERRORS OFF turn the drive mapping assignments and any related error messages off. Next, a message is written onscreen using WRITE telling the user that he or she is logging into the Acme Fireworks Company Network. A spacegun-like sound is made five times with the FIRE PHASERS 5 command. A welcome message, custom defined with the time of day and user login name is then displayed. The IF command determines whether it is Monday, Wednesday, Friday, or Saturday using system variables and displays an appropriate message.

Next, the login name is checked and if the supervisor is found, a search drive S4 is mapped to the SYSTEM directory. Otherwise S4 is not used.

The system then checks to see if the user is a member of three groups. If the user is a member, various drives are mapped to a directory for that user.

The F drive is mapped to SYS's root directory.

The G drive is mapped to the user's private directory in the HOME directory.

The H drive is mapped to APPL \ SPREADSH database program directory.

The I drive is mapped to SALES.

The J drive is mapped to the APPL \WORDPROC word processing program directory.

The K drive is mapped to the APPL \DATABASE database program directory.

The R drive is mapped to the \ADMIN data directory.

A search drive Sl is set to PUBLIC.

A search drive S2 is set to PUBLIC \%MACHINE \%OS \%OS—VERSION in order to locate the correct version of DOS command files. \% denotes the variables defined by the workstation's operating system.

A search drive S3 is set to ACCTG \PROGRAMS to locate accounting applications programs.

The DOS command PROMPT is invoked using the SET command to display the user's directory name.

A request to display DOS verification prompts is set using DOS VERIFY ON.

The Ctrl-Break key is disabled using the DOS BREAK ON command.

The COMSPEC command is used to specify which search directory (S2) is used to look for the COMMAND.COM file.

Drive G is made current using DRIVE G:

#CAPTURE is used to capture all output to printer 0 without a banner (NB), no form feed (NFF), and timeout value of five seconds (TI=5).

After the login script is executed, the menu ACME is displayed using the EXIT "MENU ACME" command.

You should now examine your system to see if a system login script exists. To call up the system login script:

TYPE/PRESS	**RESULT:**
syscon [Enter]	Displays main SYSCON menu
S [Enter]	Displays Supervisor Options menu
S [Enter]	Displays System Login Script

The systems administrator at this point should do a print screen of the information that is displayed on the screen and insert it into the systems documentation notebook.

To return to the main SYSCON menu, press Esc twice.

The next important part of your system setup is the group structure, discussed in the next section.

Listing Group Information

Users of the network can be organized into a logical category known as a *group*. Groups are often organized by department, applications, or status within the company. For example, the group ACCOUNTING could be made up of all accountants, a temporary worker, the controller, and the CEO. Once a group is established, each user name is added to it. Resources for the group such as trustee rights (limited priviledges pertaining to network files and directories) and login scripts can be specified at the same time, rather than user by user. In the group ACCOUNTING, each user can be granted identical rights to the accounting programs and data files. How to identify and alter trustee rights is discussed later in this section.

As the systems administrator, you should know what groups already exist on your system in order to be able to change group rights or add or remove certain users to and from groups. There are three important types of information you can document about groups:

- Each group name.
- The list of users in each group.
- The trustee rights assigned in each group (see "Security Trustee and Rights" in Chapter 4 for details on rights assignments).

NetWare automatically creates one group called EVERYONE. All user names added to the system are included in this group. Thus, if you want all users to have a certain set of trustee rights, you can set them for the group EVERYONE.

Figure 2.10 shows the group list for the Acme file server followed by the member list, and trustee rights.

Note that the first group is ACCTG and its member list includes USER5_ACCT, USER6_ACCT, USER7_ACCT, CAROLYN, and DENNIS. Rights for this group are assigned to the ACCTG directory.

The second group is ADMIN and its member list includes MANAGER1, MANAGER2, MANAGER3, CAROLYN, and DENNIS. Rights for this group are assigned to the directories ADMIN, ADMIN/ANALYSIS, and ADMIN/SALESDATA.

The third group is SALES and its member list includes 1_SALES, 2_SALES, 3_SALES, and 4_SALES. Rights for this group are assigned to the directories ACCTG/ORDER-DATA, SALES, SALES/LEADS, and SALES/REPORTS.

Let's identify your group names, the user lists, EVERYONE and any other group trustee rights now.

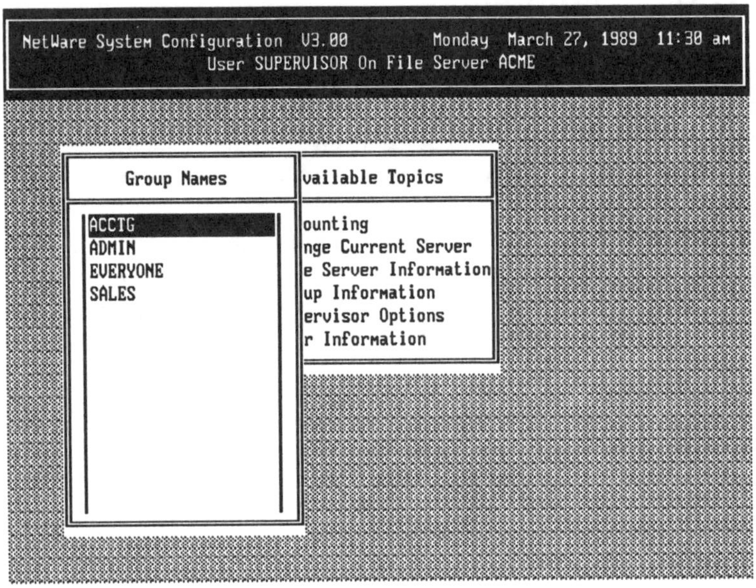

Figure 2.10 (A–F) A Groups for the Acme file server.

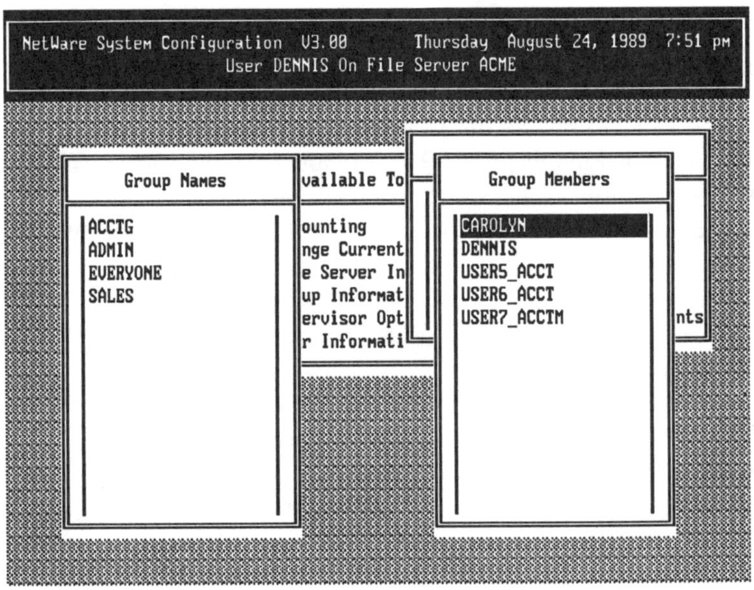

Figure 2.10B ACCTG Group Members

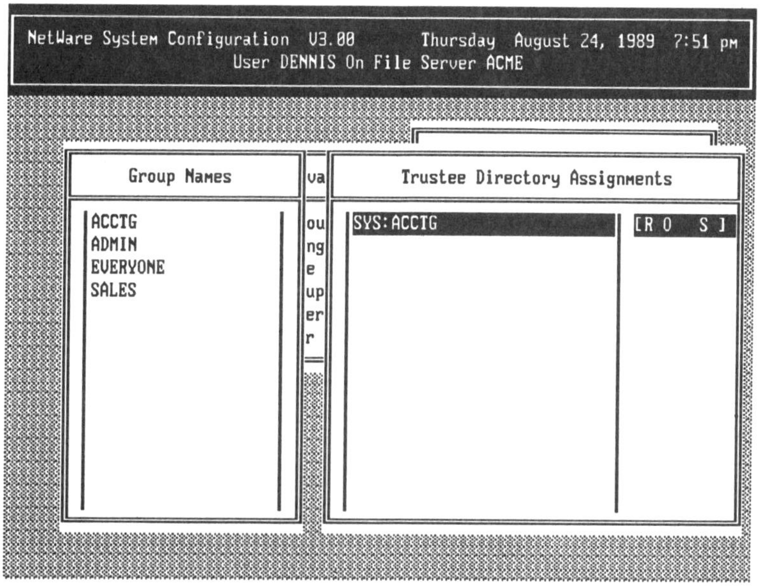

Figure 2.10C ACCTG Group Rights

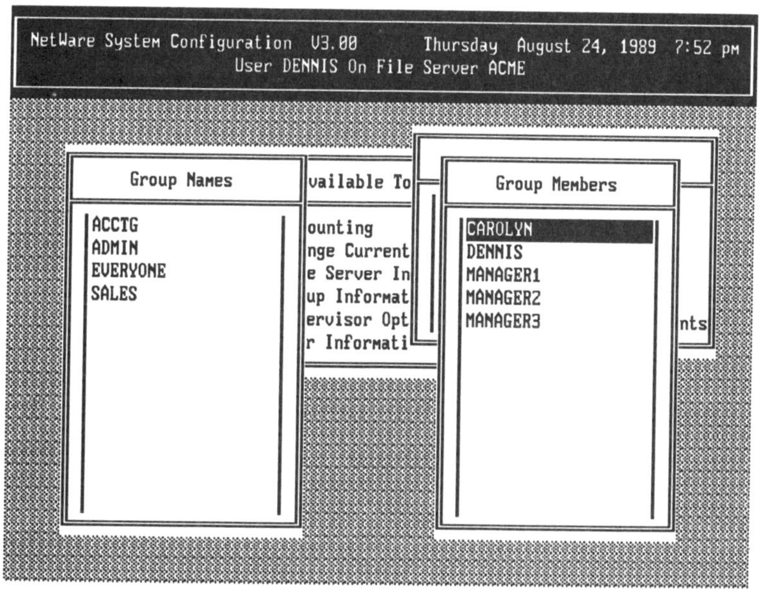

Figure 2.10D ADMIN Group Members

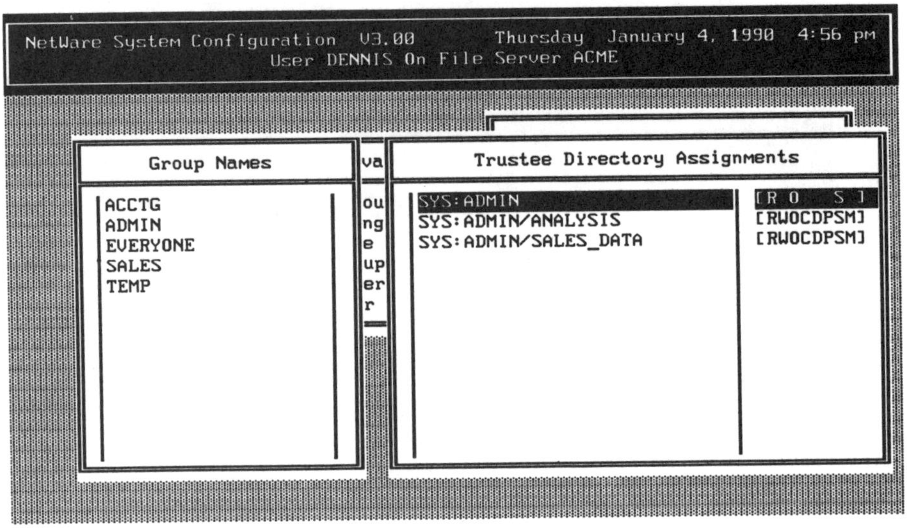

Figure 2.10E ADMIN Group Rights

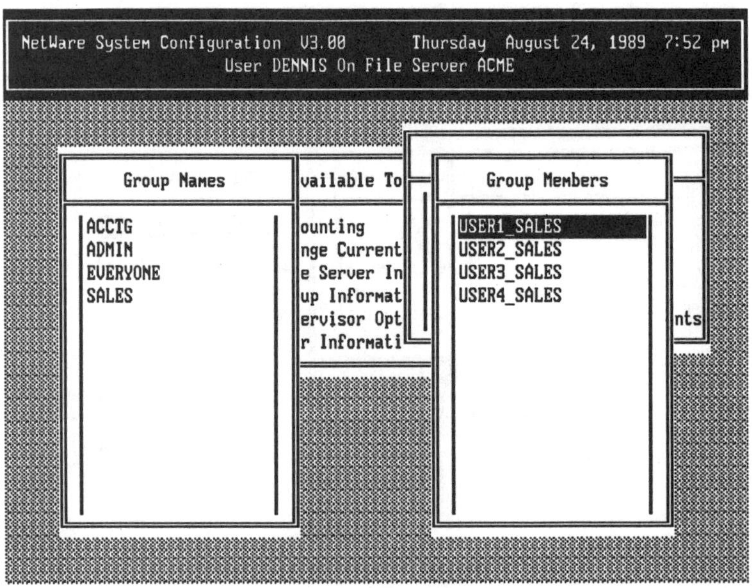

Figure 2.10F SALES Group Members

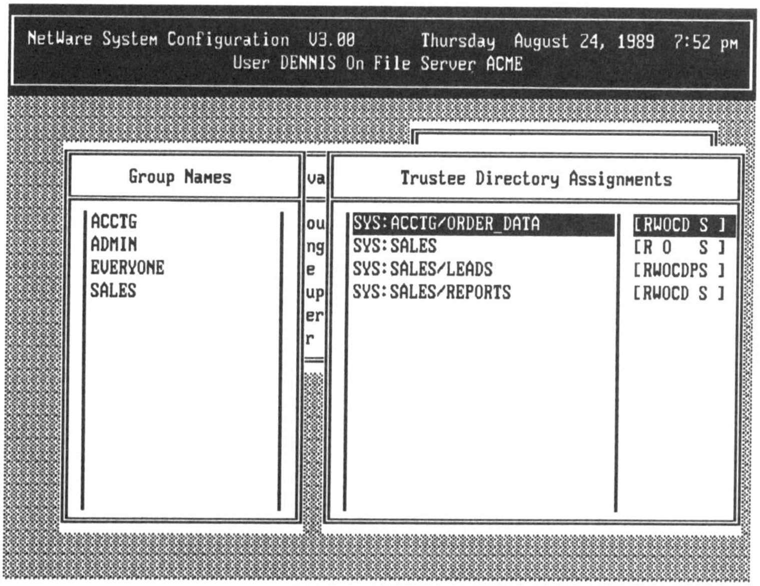

Figure 2.10G SALES Group Rights

To identify the group member list from the SYSCON menu:

TYPE/PRESS	RESULT:
G [Enter]	Selects Group Information
E [Enter]	Selects group EVERYONE
M [Enter]	Selects Member List and displays all members of group EVERYONE

You should print the information that is displayed onscreen using the shift print screen keys. This report should be inserted into your system notebook.

Now take a look at the trustee assignments for the group EVERYONE from the group member list:

TYPE/PRESS	RESULT:
Esc	Displays Group Information window
T [Enter]	Displays Trustee Assignments for group

You should print the information that is displayed onscreen using the shift print screen keys. This report should be inserted into your system notebook. Take the time now to document each group in your system in this manner.

To return to the group list from the trustee assignments:

TYPE/PRESS	RESULT:
Esc	Displays Group Information window
Esc	Displays Group Names window

Select the next group and continue the two previous printing exercises. To return to the main SYSCON menu:

TYPE/PRESS	RESULT:
Esc	Displays SYSCON main menu

The groups in your system were most likely set up by the consultant or reseller who set up the system. If the only group name displayed is the group EVERYONE, examine the needs of your users to determine whether there is a need to create a group.

You can see by our design of Acme groups how they are beneficial in organizing a system. To create a group, see the section "Creating Groups" in the "Administrative Tasks" part of this chapter.

Individual User Names, Login Scripts and Trustee Assignments

Each person who has access to the network is assigned an individual user ID that includes a password, full user name, and optional data such as an account balance, login script, and trustee assignments. This person with access is referred to as a *user*, and his or her identity can be tailored on the network to include options that apply to him or her specifically. You should be aware of each user's specific data on the network. To access a list of users on your network's current file server using SYSCON type:

TYPE/PRESS	RESULT:
SYSCON[Enter]	Displays SYSCON main menu
U[Enter]	Selects User Information option

A screen similar to Figure 2.11a and 2.11b appears. You should keep a copy of all user names documented in the systems documentation.

To display each user's login script (if any) select the user name from the SYSCON list and select Login Script. Figure 2.12a shows the individual login script for USER1_SALES.

Note that two additional search drives are mapped for SALES/LEADS and SALES/REPORTS using the next two available drive letters (*number indicates use the next available letter). Also, a menu called ACME1 is displayed after the user is logged into the system.

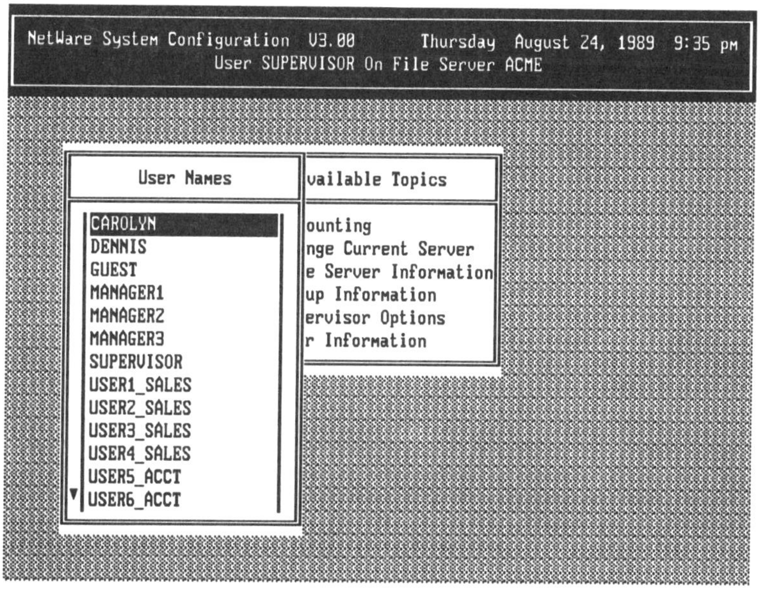

Figure 2.11a and b SYSCON user list.

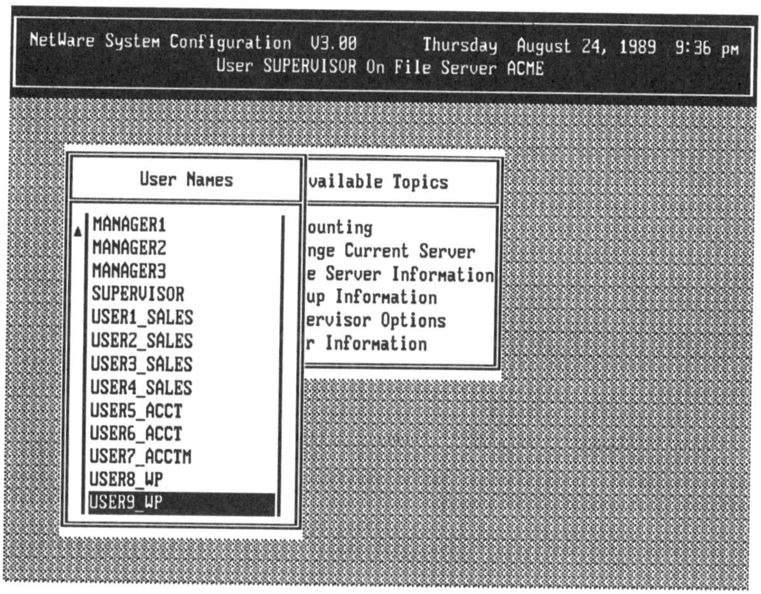

Figure 2.11b

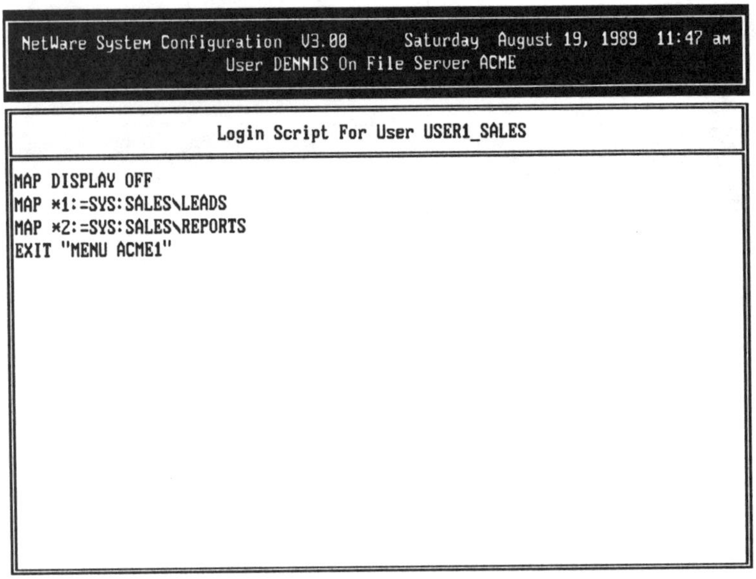

Figure 2.12 Individual login script for USER1_SALES.

Keeping a copy of user login scripts can save you time when you begin to experiment with changing their scripts. If you make changes that do not work, the copy will serve as a backup to follow if you need to restore a login script file quickly.

The last important data you should document about a user is his or her trustee rights. This is probably the most important data for a user since it ultimately determines what type of access the user has to a file server directory. Often just changing one rights assignment can cause a user to be unable to access a program or file. Figure 2.13 shows a trustee rights assignment screen for USER1_SALES.

Notice that the user has Read, Open, and Search access to the database program directory, as well as parental rights to SALES/LEADS and SALES/REPORTS. Remember that individual rights combined with group rights and each directory's maximum rights mask make up the *effective rights* for a user. If USER1_SALES did not have group parental rights to those directories, individual rights would effectively add that right to his or her mask.

However, if the directory's maximum rights mask does not include parental rights, no user other than supervisor can have parental rights in that directory.

Note that each NetWare user's trustee rights include an assignment to MAIL. **Do not** delete this directory from a user's trustee directory list, or the user will not be able to log onto the network. It is the system's way of keeping track of the user ID.

Make sure to keep a copy of each user's screen, if nothing else, to assure that correct rights assignments are used when adding new users or adding similar rights for an existing user.

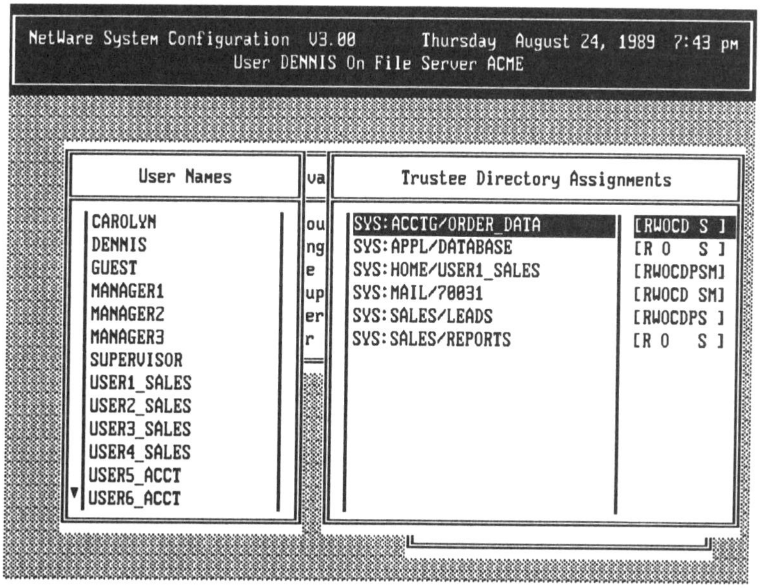

Figure 2.13 USER1_SALES trustee rights.

System Menus

NetWare versions 2.1 and above include a command utility called MENU that can be used to create custom user menus that can be invoked upon logging into the network. This menu can execute programs, present a submenu, or offer commands such as DOS or NetWare commands efficiently for users. Figure 2.14 shows the menu designed for ACME that is displayed for all users who log into the network. The section "Menu Designing" in Chapter 4 includes the actual lines entered with the MAKEUSER utility editor and further instructions and guidelines for creating menus.

Your network's systems login script will display the command:

```
exit ''menu MENUNAME''
```

if a menu is displayed for all users. Individual user login scripts may also include this line.

Most likely the file name with a .MNU is found in a PUBLIC subdirectory. If you want to print the .MNU file, type:

```
NPRINT menuname.mnu [Enter]
```

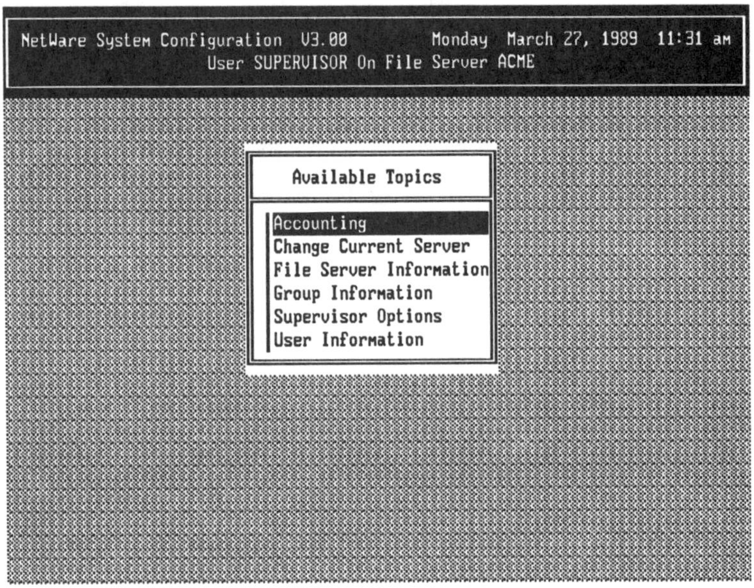

Figure 2.14 System menu on ACME file server.

Summary

In this Part 1 you have explored the basic components of the security design of your Novell NetWare network system. You have identified the file server(s), printers, and workstations. A complete inventory of all workstations has been done, and in the event of system problems, you will be able to use and provide valuable information to solve the problems. You have explored your system login script, groups, user names, and menus (if any). You should now understand the organization of your system better and be able to proceed to performing the supervisory tasks with more confidence.

Part II

Systems Administration Commands

The systems administrator's tasks on a NetWare network are divided into three groups: those that use NetWare commands, other software programs, or additional software or procedures and hardware. For example, adding a user or group and managing the network printers are administrative tasks that use NetWare commands. Other software programs such as LANSpool or Keeptrack offer the systems administrator increased network functionality such as utilizing extra printers on the network or measuring server hard disk space, respectively. Knowing how to select and use special equipment such as an uninterruptable power supply (UPS) or tape backup also is part of the systems administrator's task list. This section covers each of these task groups in the context of the tasks. It presents the appropriate commands, whether NetWare or otherwise, and the information necessary to perform each in a straightforward, easy-to-use approach. In general, the systems administrator has control over the network using the login SUPERVISOR. However, other users with equivalency to SUPERVISOR may also be interested in using these tasks.

All NetWare commands function the same for Versions 2.0 and above unless otherwise noted. There are two types of commands available to the supervisor in NetWare: Command Line Utilities and Menu Utilities. The first type is executed on a single line and looks similar to DOS commands. These commands are divided into supervisor commands (available only to the supervisor) and user commands (available to any user). All commands available to the supervisor only are discussed in each task area of Chapter 4 as follows:

ATOTAL, PAUDIT: Used by a supervisor to produce accounting statistics or records for the network. See "Accounting for Resources."

SECURITY: Used by a supervisor or consultant to determine if there are security problems in the network by looking at the bindery. See "Security and Trustee Rights" for more on using this command.

MAKEUSER: Used by a supervisor to add or delete multiple users on a regular basis using a special .USR file that stores commands. It also provides an editor to create, edit, or process the .USR file. The editor can also be used to create text files for menus. See "Adding a New User ID" and "Menu Designing" for more on using these commands.

HIDEFILE, SHOWFILE: Used by a supervisor or intermediate user to hide or show the directory listing of a file or group of files. If the file is hidden, it can not be deleted or copied over. See "Directory Management" for more on using the command.

HOLDON, HOLDOFF: Used by a supervisor to keep a file open when multiple users are accessing it to prevent overwriting of changes by each user. See "Directory Management" for more on using this command.

The general user command line utilities and the section in which they are discussed in this book are:

HELP: Accesses on-line tutorial of the NetWare commands. Use this command if you need a quick review of the NetWare commands.

ATTACH: Connects a workstation to multiple file servers. See "Logging into the Network" and "Changing File Servers."

SLIST: Lists the file servers connected to the internetwork. See "Changing File Servers."

SETPASS: Sets a user's login password. See "Adding/Changing Password."

LARCHIVE: Archives data to local disk drive. See "Backing Up."

LRESTORE: Restores data from a local drive. See "Backing Up."

NARCHIVE: Archives data to a network drive. See "Backing Up."

NRESTORE: Restores data from a network drive. See "Backing Up."

CAPTURE: Opens a file to record data for printing. Version 2.1 and above equivalency to SPOOL. See "Printer Management."

ENDCAP: Closes a file with data recorded for printing. Version 2.1 and above equivalency to ENDSPOOL. See "Printer Management."

NPRINT: Prints an ASCII text file(s). See "Printer Management."

CHKVOL: Measures the amount of disk space available on a file server volume. See "Measuring Disk Space."

FLAG: Changes file attributes. See "Directory Management—Using FILER."

LISTDIR: Views the directory structure of a volume, drive, or directory. See "File Management."

NCOPY: Copies files from one location to another. See "File Management."

NDIR: Searches globally through one or more directories for specified files or directories. See "Directory Management."

PURGE: Permanently removes files marked for deletion. See "Directory Management."

SALVAGE: Recovers deleted files that have not been purged from the system. See "Directory Management."

LOGIN: Permits user access to the network. See "Logging into the Network."

LOGOUT: Ends a user's work session on the network. See "Logging into the Network."

SYSTIME: Sets the workstation clock to the time of the file server. See "Logging into the Network."

WHOAMI: Displays your user name, file server(s) you are attached to, your connection number, and the date and time of your last login. See "Logging into the Network."

USERLIST: Lists the users currently logged on to the file server. See "Login Scripts."

MAP: Sets logical name assignments from F to Z for file server directory path names (can also map A to E to network directories). See "Mapping Logical and Search Drives."

SMODE: Shows how .COM or .EXE programs search through the system for data files. See "Mapping Logical and Search Drives."

GRANT: Assigns rights to trustees. See "Trustee Rights."

REMOVE: Removes a trustee from a directory. See "Trustee Rights."

REVOKE: Deletes trustee rights from a directory. See "Trustee Rights."

RIGHTS: Displays security rights for a user in a specific directory. See "Trustee Rights."

TLIST: Lists trustees of a directory and rights granted. See "Trustee Rights."

SEND: Sends up to 40-character messages from one user or group to another. See "Sending Messages."

CASTOFF: Disables a user from receiving messages. See "Sending Messages."

CASTON: Enables a user to receive messages. See "Sending Messages."

The following is a list of special files provided with NetWare to issue commands to attach a workstation to the network:

IPX: Loads the shell file used for internetwork package exchange (IPX.EXE). See "Shells."

NETx: Loads the NetWare shell for DOS version x at a workstation. See "Shells."

Menu utilities are commands executed through a series of menu choices. There are six that offer the supervisor specific functions:

MAKEUSER: Used by the supervisor to create, edit, or process .USR files used to add or delete users to or from the network. See "Adding a New User ID," "Creating a Group,""Deleting a User ID," or "Security and Trustee Rights."

SYSCON: Used by the supervisor for certain system configuration commands such as accounting charges and balances, adding or deleting a user or group, editing login scripts, or any other user-related commands such as changing a password, directory or file rights. See "Adding a New User ID," "Creating a Group," "Security and Trustee Rights," or "Login Scripts."

FILER: Used by the supervisor to manage directory structure or other by users for file management. See "Directory Management."

PRINTDEF, PRINTCON, and PCONSOLE: Used by the supervisor or users to perform printer configuration or by management. See "Printer Management" or "Printer Configuration."

Each of these utilities offers the supervisor powerful management functions and is discussed in the task area of Chapter 4.

Three other commands offer nonsupervisor users functions:

MENU: Used by the supervisor or users to execute menus that make access easier to applications or commands. See "Menu Designing."

SESSION: Used by the supervisor or users to control file server, default drive, logical and search drive mappings, and to identify the physical workstation number. See "Mapping Logical and Search Drives."

FCONSOLE: Used by the supervisor or console operators to access file server information and analyze network performance. See "Network Management Using FCONSOLE."

Part II demonstrates either command type under a task area heading in terms of functionality, rather than divide them into two groups as the Novell reference manual does. For example, if you are adding a new user you can use the SYSCON menu utility following a step-by-step procedure, or you can create a file with abbreviated commands using the MAKEUSER menu utility and execute a single command line utility that processes the file's commands. The section "Adding a New User ID" discusses both methods. Your Novell *Supervisor Reference* lists each command line utility alphabetically and discusses each menu utility separately. We use this approach assuming that you know the task you want to do first, and then we provide the command options available to perform it best. Each command's keyword is listed in the index at the back of the book.

There are a few general guidelines that make working with both command line and menu utilities easier. The next section provides an overview to working with each.

Chapter 3

NetWare Basics

Supervisor Command Line Utilities

These commands are available to the supervisor only because their usage by unauthorized users could cause severe problems on the network. They are executed from the DOS prompt. Once the task they perform is completed, the DOS prompt returns. They are located in the SYS:SYSTEM directory. This must be the current directory and you must be logged in as supervisor when you issue the command. You can map a drive to SYS:SYSTEM before using the command and then type *drive*:command from any directory to execute it. For example, you could map the drive H, move to another directory with a file you want to hide and type:

```
H:HIDEFILE filename [Enter]
```

Since the program files for the HIDEFILE, SHOWFILE, MAKEUSER, PAUDIT, ATOTAL, and SECURITY commands are located in the SYS:SYSTEM directory, make sure to limit access for users to this directory. If you want to make one of the utilities available to other users, copy it to another directory and assign the appropriate rights. If other users want to design their own menus, the MAKEUSER file could be copied to the PUBLIC directory.

The Command Line Utilities are divided into three categories, based on function:

Accounting

ATOTAL, PAUDIT: Used by a systems administrator to produce accounting statistics or records for the network. See "Accounting for Resources."

Security

BINDFIX, BINDREST: Used by a systems consultant to correct security problems. See the Novell *Supervisor Reference Manual*.

SECURITY: Used by a systems administrator or consultant to determine if there are security problems in the network by looking at the bindery. See "Security and Trustee Rights" for more on using this command.

MAKEUSER: Used by a systems administrator to add or delete multiple users on a regular basis using a special .USR file that stores commands. It also is a Menu Utility that provides an editor to create, edit, or process the .USR file. See "Adding a New User ID" for more on using this command.

File Management

HIDEFILE, SHOWFILE: Used by a systems administrator or intermediate user to hide or show the directory listing of a file or group of files. If the file is hidden, it can not be deleted or copied over. See "Directory Management" for more on using the command.

HOLDON, HOLDOFF: Used by a systems administrator to keep a file open when multiple users are accessing it to prevent overwriting of changes by each user. See "Directory Management" for more on using this command.

General Format Rules

When you enter a command line utility, a format similar to DOS is assumed. It includes keywords, variables, special characters, and punctuation. For example, let's use the command HIDEFILE to show each part of the format:

```
HIDEFILE [drive] [directory/] filename <[Enter]>
```

Note that brackets ([ ]) specify variables that are optional; however you do not type the brackets when executing the command. Variables that are required are shown without brackets.

The pointed brackets (< >) specify instructions that are required. For each line command, you must press the [Enter] key to complete it.

Keywords are the same as the line command name. They must be spelled correctly and typed in either lower or upper case. This book will present them in upper case for clarity. As with DOS, a space always follows the keyword if another parameter is to follow.

For example, HIDEFILE is the keyword and a space separates it from the drive, directory or filename.

Variables are the additional pieces of information you supply after the keyword. They can be optional or required and generally change each time you use the command. A space is used to separate the command from the variable.

For example, drive, directory, and filename are the variables for HIDEFILE. Drive and directory are optional variables; filename is required. If you want to use this command, the minimum information you supply is filename.

Wildcard characters (* and ?) are used the same way as in DOS. They are used to substitute characters in a filename for one or more characters. It is a common method of abbreviating a filename, performing a command on files with a common name, or searching for a filename using part of the name.

For example, if you wanted to hide all files in the current directory with an .EXE extension with the HIDEFILE command, you would type:

```
HIDEFILE *.EXE
```

This would search for all files with the extension .EXE and hide them.

Although the line commands are easy to use, they demand that you type them using a precise format. In contrast, menu commands only require you to point to the command you want and press[Enter], rather than type it. The next section discusses a menu command's general components.

Supervisor Menu Utilities

The menus offered by Novell NetWare are simple to use and very visual. They display all options, responses to options selected, and various other useful types of information. As with the command line utilities, certain commands are only available to the supervisor; others are available to users with supervisor security equivalence, a few are available to console operators, and others are available to all users. They can be invoked from any network directory by typing the menu name at the DOS prompt. A main menu for the utility will appear.

This chapter will outline all of the functions that menu utilities offer the supervisor. There are six unique supervisor menu utilities in Version 2.1: MAKEUSER, SYSCON, FILER, PRINTDEF, PRINTCON, and PCONSOLE.

There are a few basics for accessing and working with menu utilities. The first step in accessing a menu is to ensure that you are logged in as a supervisor in order to access their full power. You then type the name of the menu you wish to access followed by a [Enter] or you can type MENUMAIN to display Novell's main menu utility system, which offers a menu of all menu utilities available except MAKEUSER as shown in Figure 3.1. NetWare then displays a main menu for the command you have typed. Figure 3.2 shows the command SYSCON's main menu for Version 2.1.

Notice that the name and version of the menu utility appears in the upper left-hand corner while the date and time appear in the upper right. A centered box displays the first set of command options available. You need not memorize what each option stands for; NetWare offers on-line help for each menu.

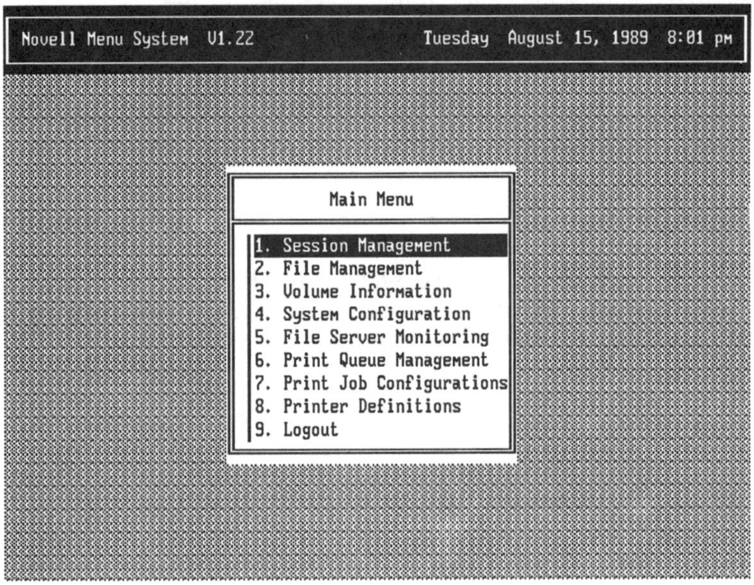

Figure 3.1 MAIN MENU display.

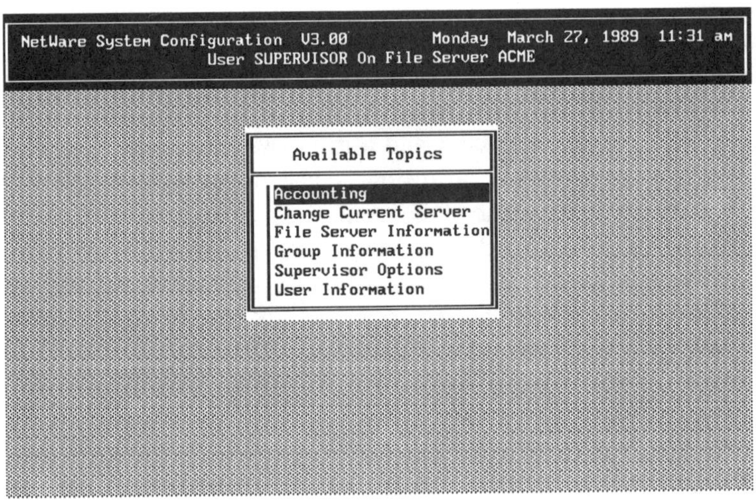

Figure 3.2 SYSCON main menu.

Accessing Help

If you are unsure about what these menu commands do or you need a quick review, press the Help key. On most keyboards, the Fl key is assigned to the Help function. Others may have a key labeled "HELP."

Once Help has been invoked, a help screen appears with appropriate information about the command you are working with. Figure 3.3 shows the help for the SYSCON main menu for Version 2.1.

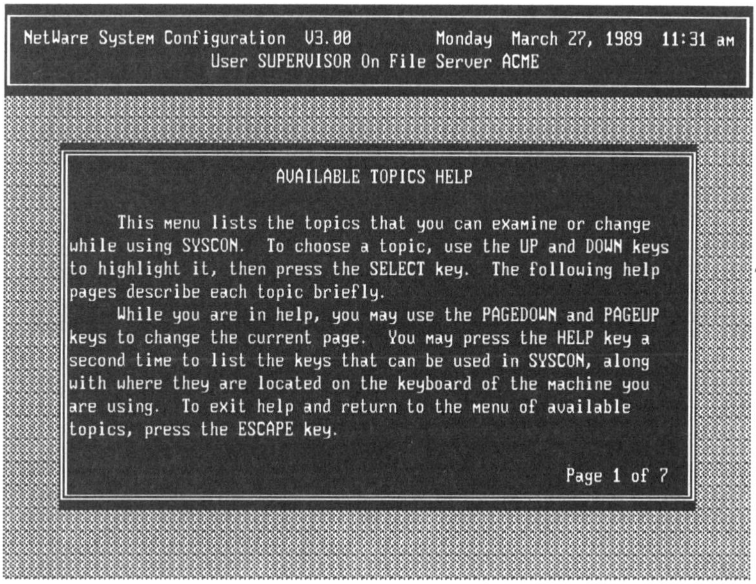

Figure 3.3 SYSCON main help screen.

In addition to the help screen describing the topic, Help also can provide a directory to which function keys are used on your keyboard to perform Novell tasks. To display this list, you press the Help key twice from any menu utility. Figure 3.4 shows an example of the function key directory for an IBM compatible keyboard for Version 2.1.

There are three screens with the list of keys assigned to functions. To access the next screen, press the PgDn key. You should do a print-screen of your function-key listing and keep it in a handy place near your keyboard.

When you are finished with the Help screen, press Esc until you return to the menu. You should now be ready to select menu options.

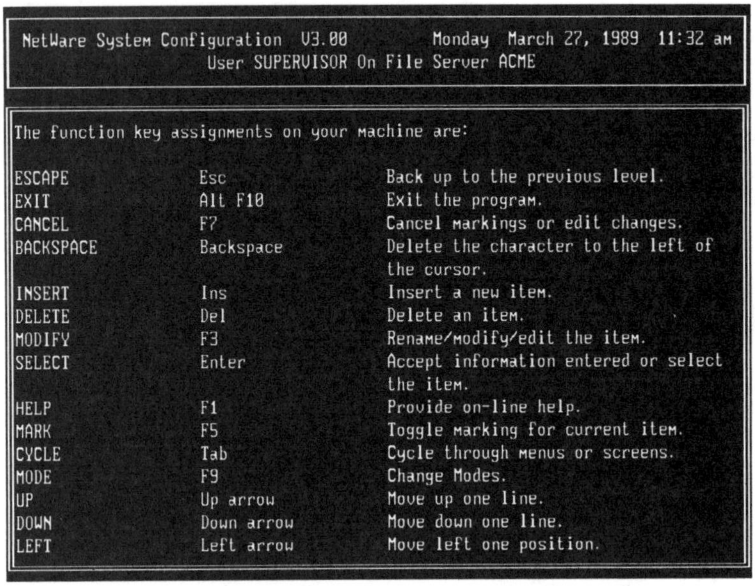

Figure 3.4 IBM Compatible function key directory.

If you are not in a menu utility, you can use the HELP command line utility to review all NetWare commands. To use this command from the DOS prompt type:

```
HELP [Enter]
```

Selecting Menu Options

To make a selection, you need only choose the option from the box or menu of options. Some menus offer lists such as user names, group names, or directory names. To select an option or item from a list, you use either the:

1. Arrow keys to move the selection bar on the option or item and press the [Enter] key.
2. First letter of an option to move the selection bar directly to the option or item and press the [Enter]. If the menu offers two or more options that begin with the same letter, press the next letter of the desired option. Continue typing the option name until it is highlighted. For example, in the FILER menu, the options "Select Current Directory" and "Set Filer Options" both begin with the letter S. To select the second option "Set Filer Options," you press S, E and T and then [Enter].

If you want to choose more than one item or option from a list, you can use the Mark key. For example, suppose you want to delete three users. You could mark each user name to delete and then press the Del key. As you mark items or options, it appears in boldface or color on most screens. The F5 key is usually the Mark key. See your function key assigned to Mark by pressing Help twice.

To reverse or unmark an item, use the Cancel key.

To move back one level in a menu utility or exit a menu utility, use the Esc key. As you leave the menu, a confirmation box will appear. You will have to type Y and press the [Enter] key to confirm that you want to exit. These boxes appear after various commands and are discussed at the end of this Chapter.

The Alt-F10 (Exit) key will take you out of a menu utility without saving any changes you have made. Take care in using this key to exit unless you are sure you don't want the changes saved.

Note: Previous versions of NetWare use the term "Select" for [Enter] or the "Enter" key as it is known on most keyboards.

Menu Utility Lists

As mentioned previously, a menu can offer lists of commands or items such as user names, group names, or other information. They may be longer than the box or contain more than one column. You can view, add, or delete information from a list of items. Figure 3.5 shows a list of users displayed from the SYSCON User Information option.

As you invoke a command that requires you to select from a list, you will be instructed on how to work with it step-by-step. Once you have used NetWare menu utilities, you will be able to apply what works with one utility to another.

Typing Additional Information in Menu Utilities

Often a command will ask you to provide more information than just a selection from a menu or list, such as a user name or password. This type of information can be entered into an *entry box*. Figure 3.6 shows an entry box for SYSCON asking for the user name.

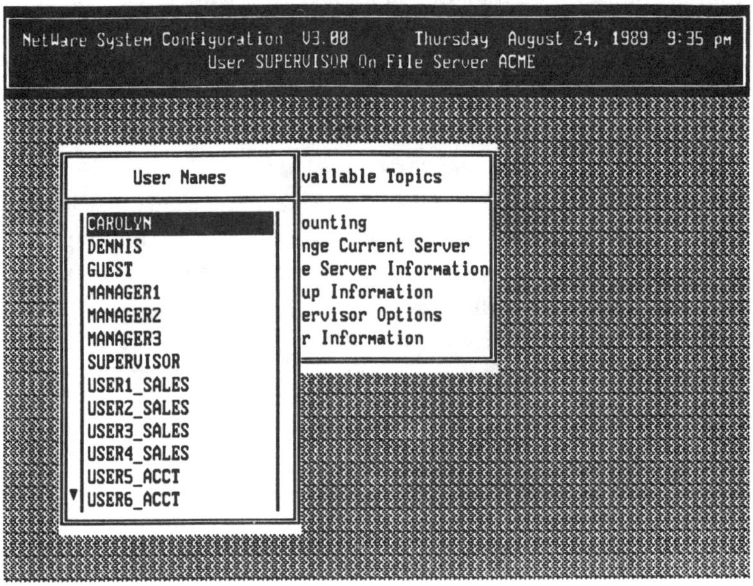

Figure 3.5 SYSCON list of users.

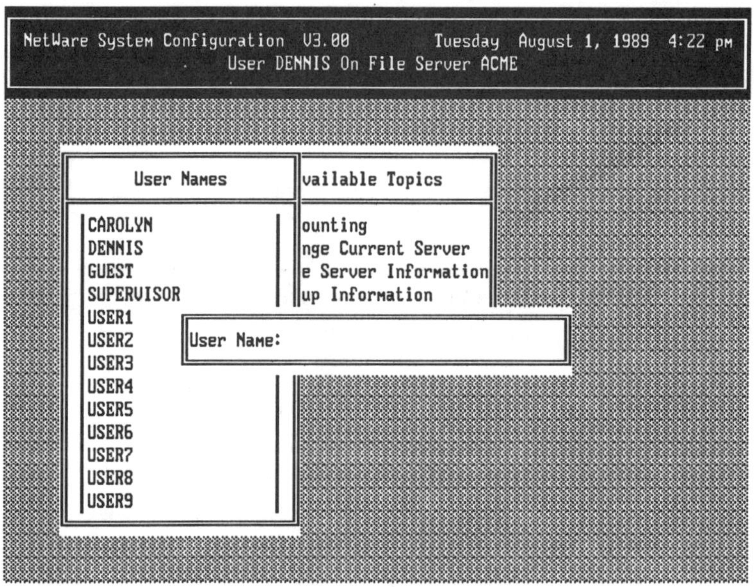

Figure 3.6 SYSCON user name entry box.

To edit characters typed in an entry box, use the DEL, Backspace, or Modify key. To complete an entry, press the [Enter] key.

Forms also offer a series of settings or fields that display information that can be changed for a command. It usually displays default or standard data in a field that can be easily changed. Figure 3.7 shows an example of a PRINTCON form.

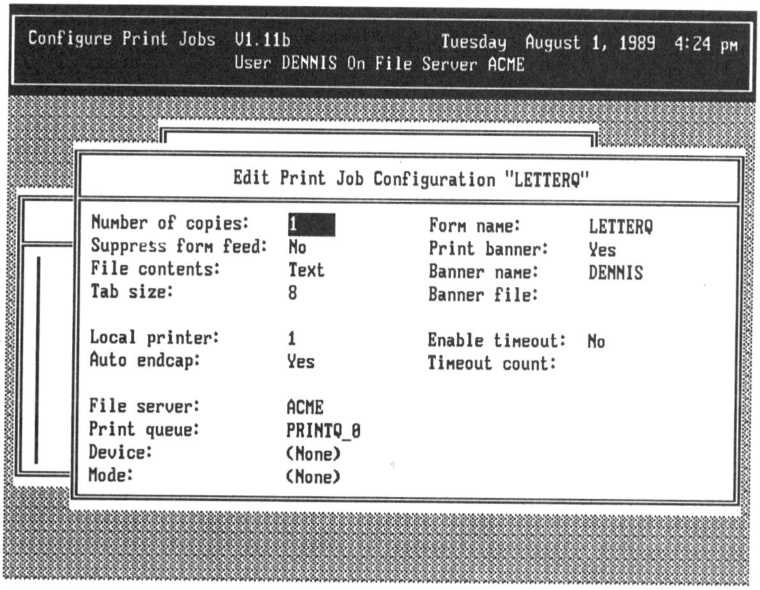

Figure 3.7 PRINTCON form.

Use the arrow keys to move from field to field in a form. Highlight the field to change, then press any letter key to see the options available. For some fields a menu may appear. Select the option you want from it.

A login script (used to store commands issued upon login for a user) is a large version of an entry box and it can use cut and paste to copy portions from other scripts. This is discussed further in "Login Scripts."

A .USR file is also a large version of an entry box used to store commands to add or delete users. It also uses a set of functions unique to it and is discussed further in "Adding a New User ID."

Viewing Additional Information in Menu Utilities

Some commands provide additional information that can not be changed. NetWare refers to this display as an *inset*. For example, the SYSCON menu offers the inset shown in Figure 3.8.

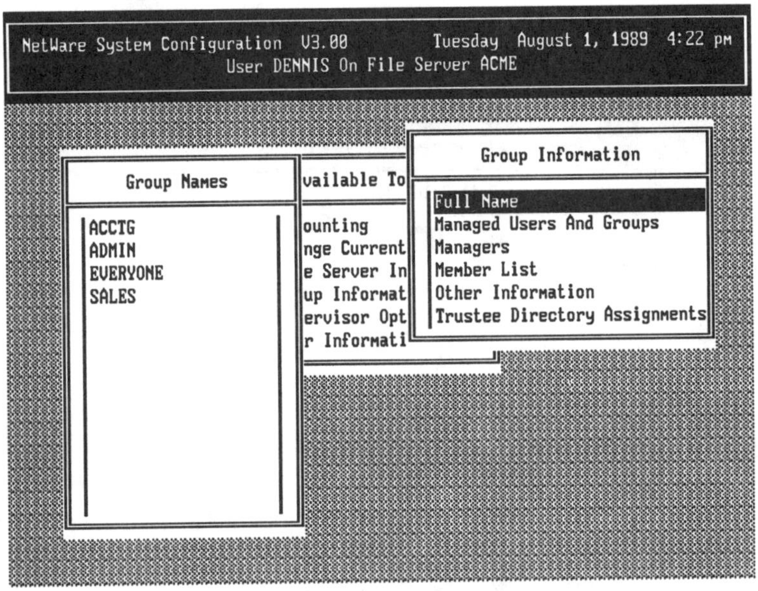

Figure 3.8 SYSCON menu inset.

This information can only be viewed or printed using the Print-Screen key or the CAPTURE command and Print-Screen key. Printing a copy on paper is a good way to document key settings on your network.

Confirmation Boxes

When you issue certain commands, NetWare displays a special warning message inside of a box known as a *confirmation box*. It is used especially after you issue commands that might prove to be nonrevokable. The box asks you to confirm that you want to issue the last command. It typically offers the command as a heading and the words "Yes" and "No." Figure 3.9 shows an example of a confirmation box from SYSCON.

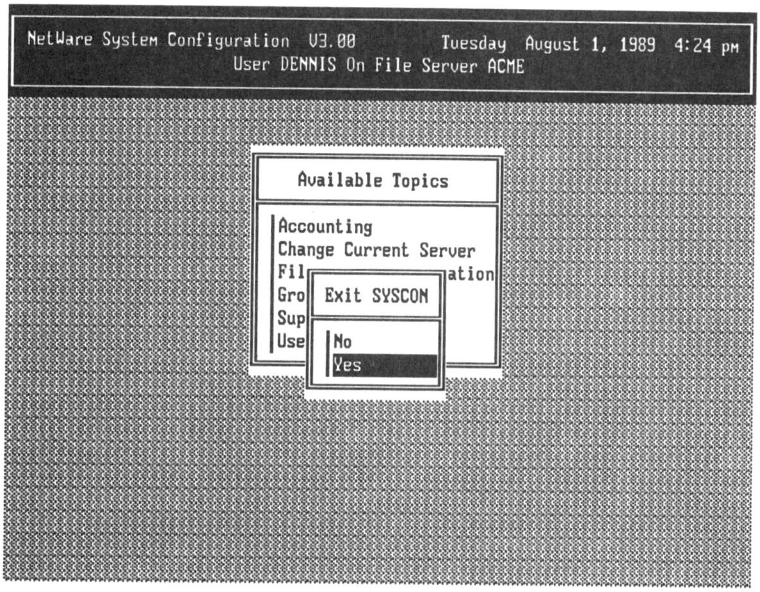

Figure 3.9 SYSCON confirmation box

You confirm or cancel the command in the box by typing Y or N and [Enter].

This is the end of the introduction to using line and menu utilities. You should now be able to understand the command keystrokes provided in the next sections. Each command assumes that you are logged in as supervisor and are operating from the DOS prompt.

Chapter 4

Network Management Tasks

Adding a New User ID

Purpose: To add a new user name to the system. SYSCON offers an easy method to add each user; MAKEUSER is more convenient when working with multiple users.

Using SYSCON

TYPE/PRESS	RESULT:
SYSCON [Enter]	Displays the SYSCON main menu
U [Enter]	Selects User Information menu
INS	Displays New User window
New user name [Enter]	Enters new user name into network
Esc	Displays SYSCON main menu
Esc	Displays Exit menu
Y [Enter]	Confirms exit from SYSCON

Using MAKEUSER

To add a new user ID with a home directory, user name, full name, password, new group (in addition to EVERYONE), trustee directory, and/or login script file

TYPE/PRESS	RESULT:
MAKEUSER [Enter]	
C [Enter]	Selects Create New USR file option
enter the following keywords:	
#GROUPS groupl[,groupN]	Creates new groups 1 to N
#LOGIN__SCRIPT filename	Creates an individual login script from filename
#HOME__DIRECTORY path directory	Creates a user home directory in path name

#CREATE user name; full name; password; groupl[,groupN]; + trustee directory namel[rights][,trustee directory name2 +[rights]]

Creates a new user with info included between ; (semicolon). To eliminate any option, leave a blank between each ;. Repeat the #CREATE line for each new user.

Esc	Completes entry of keywords
Y [Enter]	Confirms completion of entry
filename [Enter]	Specifies filename as .USR file

To process the .USR file from DOS

```
MAKEUSER filename.USR [Enter]
```

NetWare will process the commands and create the new user based on the information you have entered. This method is useful when adding multiple new users.

Adding/Changing a New Password

Purpose: To control access to the system and maintain security by requiring a user to enter a secret code for system entry.

Using SETPASS

To set your own new password from DOS

```
SETPASS [server name] [Enter]
new password [Enter]
confirm new password[Enter]
```

Using SYSCON

TYPE/PRESS	RESULT:
SYSCON [Enter]	Displays the SYSCON menu
U [Enter]	Selects User Information menu
highlight user name	Selects user name to change
[Enter]	Displays New User menu
press ↓ 2 times	Moves cursor to Change Password
[Enter]	Completes the command
new password [Enter]	Enters password for the new user
new password [Enter]	Confirms password for the new user
Esc	Displays User Name menu
Esc	Displays SYSCON main menu
Esc	Displays Exit menu
Y [Enter]	Confirms exit from SYSCON

Note: Version 2.0 does not require that you confirm the password.

Hint: You can set a password's expiration date using the login account restrictions of SYSCON. See "Login Restrictions" for more information.

Accounting for Resources

Purpose: To determine usage, charge rates, and set limits for network resources such as connect time, blocks read from or written to, server disk space, and requests made from the file server. These functions are available to Version 2.1 and above users only.

To install accounting on the file server

TYPE/PRESS	RESULT:
SYSCON [Enter]	Displays SYSCON menu
A [Enter]	Selects Accounting option
I [Enter]	Selects Install Accounting option
Y [Enter]	Selects Yes

Note: If accounting is already installed, the Install Accounting window will not appear. If not, it appears automatically.

The main accounting menu looks like Figure 4.1.

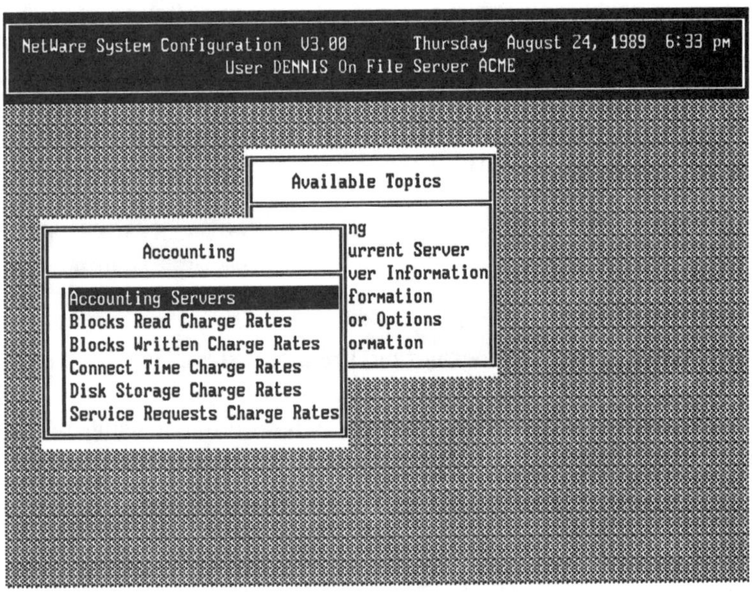

Figure 4.1 Accounting Menu.

Using ATOTAL: Measuring Daily and Weekly Resource Usage

Purpose: Determines total usage of accounting services and assists in establishing charge rates. Produces summary total statistics for blocks read and written, connect time in minutes, service requests, and disk storage in blocks/day on a daily or weekly basis as shown in Table 4.1. Information can be displayed to the screen or a filename. Accounting must be installed on the server with test charges set for services.

Table 4.1 Sample ATOTAL statistic display

06/26/1989:			
Connect time:	7750	Server requests:	114598
Blocks read:	12141	Blocks written:	759
Blocks days:	1200		
06/27/1989:			
Connect time:	4159	Server requests:	123069
Blocks read:	12850	Blocks written:	1887
Blocks days:	1450		
06/28/1989:			
Connect time:	7510	Server requests:	177110
Blocks read:	16222	Blocks written:	1693
Blocks days:	1000		
06/29/1989:			
Connect time:	5430	Server requests:	313133
Blocks read:	29637	Blocks written:	18913
Blocks days:	900		
06/30/1989:			
Connect time:	5705	Server requests:	72838
Blocks read:	4127	Blocks written:	131
Blocks days:	900		
Totals for week:			
Connect time:	30554	Server requests:	800748
Blocks read:	74977	Blocks written:	23383
Blocks days:	5450		

To produce the ATOTAL usage report, test charges must be set for each service you want to measure usage for. We recommend a rate of 1/1 that charges a unit for each service's usage. To set actual charges for a service based on an estimated cost per week and the ATOTAL actual usage statistics, see the appropriate "Setting Charges" section that follows. Figure 4.2 shows the screen used to set charges for each service from SYSCON.

```
NetWare System Configuration  V3.00        Thursday  August 24, 1989  6:34 pm
                        User DENNIS On File Server ACME

                                                 Sun  Mon  Tue  Wed  Thu  Fri  Sat
    Blocks Read Charge Rates             8:00am   1    1    1    1    1    1    1
                                         8:30am   1    1    1    1    1    1    1
                                         9:00am   1    2    2    2    2    2    1
Sunday                                   9:30am   1    2    2    2    2    2    1
8:00 am To 8:29 am                      10:00am   1    1    1    1    1    1    1
                                        10:30am   1    1    1    1    1    1    1
Rate  Charge        Rate  Charge        11:00am   1    1    1    1    1    1    1
 1  No Charge        11                 11:30am   1    1    1    1    1    1    1
 2  1/1              12                 12:00pm   1    1    1    1    1    1    1
 3                   13                 12:30pm   1    1    1    1    1    1    1
 4                   14                  1:00pm   1    1    1    1    1    1    1
 5                   15                  1:30pm   1    1    1    1    1    1    1
 6                   16                  2:00pm   1    1    1    1    1    1    1
 7                   17                  2:30pm   1    1    1    1    1    1    1
 8                   18                  3:00pm   1    1    1    1    1    1    1
 9                   19                  3:30pm   1    1    1    1    1    1    1
10                   20                  4:00pm   1    1    1    1    1    1    1
       (Charge is per block)             4:30pm   1    1    1    1    1    1    1
```

Figure 4.2 Accounting set charges screen.

To set test charges for connect time, block reads, block writes, or file server requests using SYSCON

TYPE/PRESS	RESULT:
SYSCON [Enter]	Displays SYSCON menu
A [Enter]	Selects Accounting option
select the service from the menu [Enter]	Selects service to set charge for
→ to select Monday 8:00 a.m.	
F5 (Mark key)	Specifies Monday 8:00 a.m. as first day and hour to begin charges from
→ ↓ to select Friday 5:00 p.m. [Enter]	Specifies Friday 5:00 p.m. as last day and hour to end charges

O [Enter]	Selects Other Charge Rate option
1 (or other #) [Enter]	Specifies multiplier
1 (or other #) [Enter]	Specifies divisor
Esc	Saves charge setting

To set test charges for disk storage using SYSCON:

TYPE/PRESS	RESULT:
SYSCON [Enter]	Displays SYSCON menu
A [Enter]	Selects Accounting option
↓ [Enter]	Selects Disk Storage option
↓ to select Sunday 2:00 a.m.	
F5 (Mark key)	Specifies Sunday 2:00 a.m. as first day and hour to begin charges from
→ to select Saturday 2:00 a.m.	Specifies Saturday 2:00 a.m. as last day
[Enter]	and hour to end charges
O [Enter]	Selects Other Charge Rate option
1 (or other #) [Enter]	Specifies multiplier
1 (or other #) [Enter]	Specifies divisor
Esc	Saves charge setting

Now that the test rates are set, ATOTAL can be used on a weekly basis to produce usage statistics.

To display the statistics from the SYS:SYSTEM directory

```
ATOTAL [Enter]
```

To save the statistics to a file

```
ATOTAL>filename [Enter]
```

You should repeat this process for a few weeks to gather the data needed for each service. An average or maximum over the period could be used as the estimated usage for each service.

To estimate a cost for each service you could take the total cost of the system and charge users over the first year. The following example data shows how one method could be used to establish a total cost per week.

Total System Cost:	$150,000
Total Weeks:	50
Cost/Week	=$150,000/50
	=$3,000

You could then determine which services you want to charge for each week. If you want to charge for all services, an example charge per week per service could be:

Connect Time:	$ 500
File Server Requests:	$ 800
Block Read Charges:	$ 200
Block Write Charges:	$1,000
Disk Space Charges:	$ 500
Total	$3,000

You could select only connect time and disk space and charge equally for them. Once weekly charges are determined, a rate can be set based on charges per week and usage.

Setting Connect Time Charges Using SYSCON

To set test charges for connect time using SYSCON

TYPE/PRESS	RESULT:
SYSCON [Enter]	Displays SYSCON menu
A [Enter]	Selects Accounting option
C [Enter]	Selects Connect Time option
→ to select Monday 8:00 a.m.	
F5 (Mark key)	Specifies Monday 8:00 a.m. as first day and hour to begin charges from
→ ↓ to select Friday 5:00 p.m.	Specifies Friday 5:00 p.m. as last day

[Enter]	and hour to end charges
O [Enter]	Selects Other Charge Rate option
$ charge per week x 100	Specifies weekly charge in cents as numerator of rate calculation
estimated usage in units (from ATOTAL)	Specifies weekly usage estimate as divisor of rate calculation
[Enter]	Computes rate to charge
Esc	Saves charge settings

You may want to document the charge per week and usage since NetWare computes the rate, and the inputs used are not stored.

Setting File Server Request Charges Using SYSCON

To set test charges for file server requests using SYSCON

TYPE/PRESS	RESULT:
SYSCON [Enter]	Displays SYSCON menu
A [Enter]	Selects Accounting option
F [Enter]	Selects File Server Requests option
→ to select Monday 8:00 a.m. F5 (Mark key)	Specifies Monday 8:00 a.m. as first day and hour to begin charges from
→ ↓ DA to select Friday 5:00 p.m. [Enter]	Specifies Friday 5:00 p.m. as last day and hour to end charges
O[Enter]	Selects Other Charge Rate option
$ charge per week x 100	Specifies weekly charge in cents as numerator of rate calculation
estimated usage in units (from ATOTAL)	Specifies weekly usage estimate as divisor of rate calculation
[Enter]	Computes rate to charge
Esc	Saves charge settings

You may want to document the charge per week and usage since NetWare computes the rate and the original inputs used are not stored.

Setting Block Read Charges Using SYSCON

To set test charges for block reads using SYSCON

TYPE/PRESS	RESULT:
SYSCON [Enter]	Displays SYSCON menu
A [Enter]	Selects Accounting option
B [Enter]	Selects Block Reads option
→ to select Monday 8:00 a.m.	
F5 (Mark key)	Specifies Monday 8:00 a.m. as first day and hour to begin charges from
→ ↓ to select Friday 5:00 p.m. [Enter]	Specifies Friday 5:00 p.m. as last day and hour to end charges
O [Enter]	Selects Other Charge Rate option
$ charge per week x 100	Specifies weekly charge in cents as numerator of rate calculation
estimated usage in units (from ATOTAL)	Specifies weekly usage estimate as divisor of rate calculation
[Enter]	Computes rate to charge
Esc	Saves charge settings

You may want to document the charge per week and usage since NetWare computes the rate and the original inputs used are not stored.

Setting Block Write Charges Using SYSCON

To set test charges for block writes using SYSCON

TYPE/PRESS	RESULT:
SYSCON [Enter]	Displays SYSCON menu
A [Enter]	Selects Accounting option
B [Enter]	Selects Block Writes option

→ to select Monday 8:00 a.m. F5 (Mark key)	Specifies Monday 8:00 a.m. as first day and hour to begin charges from
→ ↓ to select Friday 5:00 p.m. [Enter]	Specifies Friday 5:00 p.m. as last day and hour to end charges
O [Enter]	Selects Other Charge Rate option
$ charge per week x 100	Specifies weekly charge in cents as numerator of rate calculation
estimated usage in units (from ATOTAL)	Specifies weekly usage estimate as divisor of rate calculation
[Enter]	Computes rate to charge
Esc	Saves charge settings

You may want to document the charge per week and usage since NetWare computes the rate and the original inputs used are not stored.

Setting Disk Space Charges Using SYSCON

To set test charges for disk storage using SYSCON:

TYPE/PRESS	RESULT:
SYSCON [Enter]	Displays SYSCON menu
A [Enter]	Selects Accounting option
D [Enter]	Selects Disk Storage option
↓ to select Sunday 2:00 a.m. F5 (Mark key)	Specifies Sunday 2:00 a.m. as first day and hour to begin charges from
→ to select Saturday 2:00 a.m. [Enter]	Specifies Saturday 2:00 a.m. as last day and hour to end charges
O [Enter]	Selects Other Charge Rate option
$ charge per week x 100	Specifies weekly charge in cents as numerator of rate calculation

estimated usage in units (from ATOTAL)	Specifies weekly usage estimate as divisor of rate calculation
[Enter]	Computes rate to charge
Esc	Saves charge settings

Setting Default and Individual User Account Balances Using SYSCON

The user account balance can be set two ways

- Use a default for all users.
- Use an individual limit for each user.

The default system screen looks like Figure 4.3.

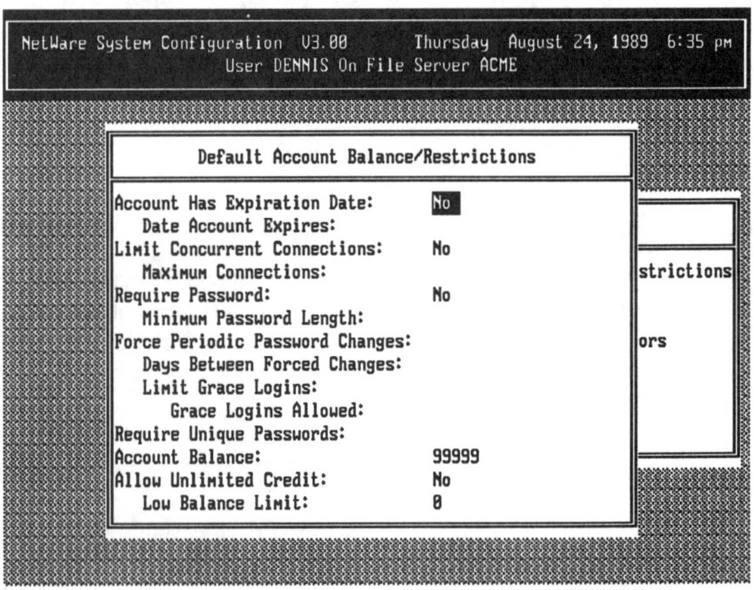

Figure 4.3 Default user account balance screen.

To set the system default for all users

TYPE/PRESS	RESULT:
SYSCON [Enter]	Displays SYSCON menu
S [Enter]	Selects Supervisor Options
D [Enter]	Selects Default Account Balance option
move to Account Balance [Enter]	Selects Account Balance setting
default value [Enter]	Sets the default account balance
move to Allow Unlimited Credit [Enter]	Selects the Allow Credit setting
Y [Enter]	Specifies that users have unlimited credit
or	
N [Enter]	Specifies that users have limited credit
move to Lower Balance Limit [Enter]	Selects Lower Balance Limit
value [Enter]	Specifies a positive balance or negative balance as lower limit
Esc	Saves settings

To set an account balance for an individual user

TYPE/PRESS	RESULT:
SYSCON [Enter]	Displays SYSCON menu
U [Enter]	Selects User Information option
select user name [Enter]	Selects user to set balance for
A [Enter]	Selects Account Balance option
move to Account Balance [Enter]	Selects Account Balance setting
value [Enter]	Sets the user's account balance
move to Allow Unlimited Credit [Enter]	Selects the Allow Credit setting
Y or [Enter]	Specifies that user has unlimited credit
N [Enter]	Specifies that user has limited credit
move to Lower Balance Limit [Enter]	Selects Lower Balance Limit
value [Enter]	Specifies a positive balance or negative balance as lower limit
Esc	Saves settings

NetWare will now keep track of account balances for the user. If a user runs out of available charges, he or she will not be able to access the network until the charges are reset by the supervisor.

Using PAUDIT: Examining System Accounting Records

Purpose: Views the system accounting records stored in the audit file NET$ACCT.DAT. Each time a user logs in or out of the file server, a record is written to this file. Figure 4.4 shows an example of a group of records from the audit file.

```
4/1/89 13:32:48 File Server ACME
 NOTE: about User DENNIS during File Server services.
 Login from address 00000001:000000000091.
4/1/89 13:33:31 File Server ACME
 NOTE: about User DENNIS during File Server services.
 Logout from address 00000001:000000000091.
4/1/89 13:33:31 File Server ACME
 NOTE: about User DENNIS during File Server services.
 Login from address 00000001:000000000091.
4/1/89 13:34:29 File Server ACME
 NOTE: about User DENNIS during File Server services.
 Logout from address 00000001:000000000091.
4/1/89 13:34:29 File Server ACME
 NOTE: about User DENNIS during File Server services.
 Login from address 00000001:000000000091.
4/1/89 16:19:11 File Server ACME
 NOTE: about File Server ACME during File Server services.
 System time changed to 1989-08-01 16:19:11.
8/1/89 16:19:50 File Server ACME
 CHARGE: 1577559 to User SUPERVISOR for File Server services.
 12804 disk blocks stored for 5914 half-hour periods.
8/1/89 16:19:51 File Server ACME
 CHARGE: 3627499 to User DENNIS for File Server services.
 29442 disk blocks stored for 5914 half-hour periods.
Z::\ PUBLIC\ SHARE>
```

Figure 4.4 Sample PAUDIT-generated audit file records.

To display actual charges for all users from the SYS:SYSTEM directory:

```
PAUDIT [Enter]
```

Hint: To send the output of ATOTAL or PAUDIT to a file, type:

```
ATOTAL>filename  [Enter]
or
PAUDIT>filename [Enter]
```

To print a file to a printer, type

```
NPRINT filename  [Enter]
```

To view the contents of a large file one screen at a time, type

```
TYPE filename | MORE  [Enter]
```

The disadvantage of this command is that the data includes login and logout connections chronologically for each user in between charges. You should erase the NET$ACCT.DAT file after each week's charges are computed or the file will continue to save each week's statistics. You could use the > filename option with this command to write the statistics (stored in binary) to an ASCII file.

Once in this format, you could write an accounting program using database software, use a word processing or text editor program to search for CHARGE and transfer the data to a spreadsheet, or purchase a third-party program to handle the compilation of a charge summary by user.

Backing Up the System

Purpose: To protect the network from common types of disasters that halt operation. Steps to ensuring against crisis include:

- Keep spare and backup components.
- Guard against natural disasters.
- Maintain a backup power supply for key hardware.
- Consider a stand-by power supply.
- Purchase a surge protector at minimum for other hardware.
- Select the appropriate backup medium.
- Perform repeated backups.
- Practice restoring from backup medium.

Spare and Backup Components

You should have at least one workstation that could take the place of the file server if necessary. This workstation doesn't have to have the same amount of storage as the regular file server, but it should have enough to keep the key functions available on the system until the main unit is repaired. Keep a LAN parts kit that includes at least one workstation NIC (network interface card), one file server NIC (if they are different), and any other major system components—active hubs, passive hubs, bridge devices, gateway, cards, etc. Although this is a significant expenditure, in comparison to possible down time of several days for all of the users, it is a small price to pay.

Natural Disasters

Every user should be aware of the chance of fire damage to the LAN file server and be able to turn off equipment that is smoking or burning before the overhead sprinklers turn on. A hand-held halogen extinguisher should be readily available to all users near the file server. The file server should not be located under an overhead sprinkler system head. Sprinkler heads located in the same room should be restricted from directly spraying on the file server.

Ensuring Backup Power Using a UPS

Every systems administrator should be aware of the possibility of a major power outage and the problems this can cause. Over 275,000 PCs and workstations experience hardware damage by spikes and surges each year. More than 50 percent of all service calls can be traced to power related problems. In fact, most of the Fortune 100 MIS managers say power problems have cost them more money than other problems. If you would survey most of the electrical utilities around the country, you would find that most, if not all, do not guarantee disturbance-free power 100 percent of the time. A systems administrator should make sure that the network is protected against power disturbances as well as possible. The best way to ensure against power loss is through the use of a *UPS* (Uninterruptible Power Supply).

A UPS is a device that supplies an alternative power supply to the devices connected to it. The unit contains a transformer that charges the batteries used to provide the power and a voltage regulator that examines power constantly. You should select a UPS designed for a file server application. Its backup power rating needs to be properly sized at no less than 80 percent of UPS capacity. To determine your wattage needs you can use the following formula:

Total Volts x Total Amps x .48 (of all connected devices)	=	Wattage needed for your backup power supply

Note: If you have one file server with one internal hard disk, a 400 watt UPS will last about 20 minutes; a 700 watt UPS will last about 30 minutes. As you add devices to the UPS, the time that the UPS will stay up in the event of a power loss or inconsistency decreases.

Both the file server and the workstation that has the tape or other backup unit should be connected to the UPS. In the event of a complete power outage, you will then be able to close any open files and bring the server down with as little impact on the data as possible.

In addition to the file server, other devices that should be protected include workstations that are being used as bridges, hubs, repeaters, or wire centers.

Any device that could be the cause of a catastrophic data loss should be protected by a UPS or a standby power supply. If the budget allows, you could have a UPS on every workstation. This would give you complete network electrical protection. UPSs range in price from $900 to $2000. Cost is usually determined by the wattage of the unit and the amount of time the unit will keep the devices connected to it running during a power loss. The higher the wattage rating and the longer the time, the higher the price. The wattage rating determines the amount of power the unit supplies; the time limit is the length in minutes or hours it will supply backup power. The longer the time limit supplied by a UPS, the more tasks you can do within the network, such as closing accounting systems, doing tape backups, and finishing works in progress.

Some important features to look for in a UPS are:

- Provides voltage regulation of at least +5 percent of total voltage required.
- Supports file server communications for unattended shut down.
- Has a compatible output wave shape (adapted to correct frequency; 60 hz in U.S., 55 hz in Europe).
- Automatic restart when power is restored.
- Hard battery disconnect when power is restored.
- Electronic overload protection.
- Automatic battery recharge up to 4 hours.

Alternative Power Protection: Standby Power Supply

Another type of backup power device is a an *SPS* (standby power supply). Standby power supplies provide adequate protection from surges, spikes, EMI/RFI noise as well as excellent protection from blackouts and brownouts. An SPS is slightlyless expensive than a true UPS and is an economical solution for critical workstations, tape subsystems, gateways, bridges, or nodes doing distributed processing. (SPSs, however, have a time lag when transferring from the line voltage to battery-invertor voltage.)

Some features to look for in an SPS are:

- Power rating at least 125 percent of power needs.
- Minimum 100 joules surge protection on all three incoming legs (Line, Neutral, and Ground).
- EMI/RFI filtering on all three incoming legs.
- AC to invertor transfer time of under 10 milliseconds.
- Automatic battery recharge of less than 8 hours.
- Compatible output wave shape.
- Support for UPS monitoring.
- Automatic restart when power is restored.
- Hard battery disconnect when power is restored.
- Electronic overload protection.

Protecting Workstations: High Performance Surge Suppressors

Surge suppressors are good at countering another electrical fact. High and low dips in power, power surges and spikes, and noise can affect network performance as well. If you have a UPS on all of your network equipment, these types of electrical inconsistencies are handled. If not, you can protect against electrical problems such as these by the addition of a high quality line conditioner and surge protectors. These products are fairly inexpensive for the protection they provide. Prices range from $25 to $100. Make sure that you purchase high quality devices and devices that protect all three legs of the line.

Other features to look for in a surge protector are:

- High level of surge protection for all three incoming legs (Line, Neutral, Ground).
- Lightning arrestor (automatic disconnect).
- Rapid response, less than 5 nanoseconds at 200 volts peak.
- EMI/RFI filtering for both high and low frequencies.
- Modem line surge suppression when necessary.
- Wiring diagnostics.
- Low voltage alarm.

Backing Up the LAN

One of the most important data security tools is the system or network backup. There are several means of producing an effective and secure backup of your data. The most important responsibility of the systems administrator is to perform a daily backup. You may sometimes be tempted to think of a primary storage failure as a terrible tragedy that always happens to "the other guy." But remember the other guy could turn out to be you. There is nothing worse than having your system crash and then realizing that you don't have a current backup.

System files

The system files are the file server security files that contain lists of users, groups, passwords, security equivalences, full names, and ID numbers. They are hidden files located in the directory SYSTEM; NET$BIND.SYS, and NET$BVAL.SYS (you can't see them by typing a DIR at the SYSTEM prompt). It is very important that these files are backed up on a regular basis. Whenever you add or delete a user or group or make changes in the trustee rights of your system's users, these files are altered. Before you make a decision about a backup unit, make sure that it can back up the Novell system files.

Frequency of Backup

You should have a written procedure on how you want the network to be backed up. Only you know the importance of your business' data. Some businesses will need to back up the whole system every day, others will only want to back up the data that has been modified since the last backup, and still others will only need to back up the data files on a regular basis. The section that follows gives you an example of a recommended backup procedure. You can modify it to fit your own business needs. Remember that your business counts on this system's reliability and therefore the data is vital to you. It is better to back up frequently than to have a system crash and not have a current backup. A nonexistent backup or one that is outdated means that you must rebuild the system or rebuild it from the point of the last backup. Consider how many long hours this would take compared to spending one or two hours to ensure your network data is recoverable.

The first recommended backup procedure would be to back up everyday in this order: You would have three sets of backup media—day one, day two, and day three. These are known as Grandfather, Father, and Son backups. On Monday you use Grandfather media and do a full system backup. That media will be stored in a safe place, preferably in a fireproof safe or file cabinet. On Tuesday you use Father media to do a full backup and store it in a safe place. On Wednesday you use Son media to do a full backup and also store it in a safe place. On Thursday you use Grandfather media and do a full backup and so on, repeating the procedure until the end of the week, at which time you do two system backups and take one set of media offsite. The offsite media will be rotated each week.

If your data does not change very often you could change the procedure to back up only those files that have been modified since the last backup and then do a complete backup at the end of the week. Again using the Grandfather, Father, Son procedure as listed above.

The third type of backup would be to back up only the data files, using the above procedure of Grandfather, Father, and Son.

No matter which backup procedure you decide to use for your system, the most important thing to remember is to do the backup, check to make sure it worked, and test periodically restoring a file from the backup medium to a local disk.

Local Drive Backup Medium and Procedures

The first and least expensive media are floppy disks in a disk drive, either A: or B:, a fixed local hard disk C:, or a removable hard drive cartridge such as a Bernoulli system. If you use floppy disks or Bernoulli cartridges, you will most likely have to attend the backup to insert new diskettes or cartridges as they fill up. Remember that files users are working on during the backup will be open and thus not backed up.

With any of these three media, you use the Novell NetWare utility called LARCHIVE. To use LARCHIVE, you must be logged into the file server from a workstation and you should have all rights to all files and directories (supervisor rights or the equivalent).

To back up using LARCHIVE from the F prompt

TYPE/PRESS	**RESULT:**
LARCHIVE [Enter]	LARCHIVE System Prompt will appear: You must be a supervisor in order to perform a complete system

	backup. If you are not a supervisor, only directories to which you have rights can be backed up. Back up fixed volume SYS? (Y/N)
Y	Enter the letter of the local disk drive on which to archive files:
A,B	To back up to disk drive A or B
or	
C,D,E	To back up to hard disk C, D, or E
	Do you want to print a log report of this session? (Y/N)
N	

Note: The log report is actually a file called ARCHIVE.LOG created by LARCHIVE and stored with the other archive files. It includes date and time of archiving session, the directory path of each directory from which you archive one or more files, a list of all archive files.

	No log will be printed (you can always print a copy of the log later by using NPRINT ARCHIVE.LOG Select specific directories to be backed up? (N=Back up all directories)
N	
	Select the backup mode for this directory from the following:
	1. Back up ALL qualified files in each directory 2. Back up ONLY qualified files that have been modified since last backup
1 or 2	
	1. Select specific files 2. Ignore specific files 3. Back up all files
1 or 2 or 3	
	SYS:SYSTEM If you are archiving to a floppy disk

drive (or other removable media) insert a diskette. Press the space bar to continue.

space

LARCHIVE will now archive all specified files from all specified directories and subdirectories to the local drive you specified (either to floppy diskettes or to a local hard disk).

When the specified files are archived, the following message will appear:

```
''Archive Session Completed.''
```

Using LRESTORE

The LRESTORE command is used to copy data backed up with LARCHIVE to another drive or the file server. An LRESTORE command session involves defining where your backup data is, what parts of that data you want to restore, and where you want to restore the data. LRESTORE gets all this information from you by prompting you at the command line. Like LARCHIVE, LRESTORE allows you to set up filters for selecting directories. However LRESTORE doesn't do the same for files, which you must select or skip individually. The typical LRESTORE session is a completely interactive one.

LRESTORE can restore the entire file server's directory structure in the case of a complete primary storage failure. You will be prompted to restore each file. If you want to restore one file, confirm with "Yes." LRESTORE is reliable but not as easy to use as a tape backup system and accompanying software.

Tape Backup Systems

A second backup medium available is the cassette tape that uses a special tape backup unit. With Novell NetWare, you are provided with the capability of accessing a large amount of data storage in a nonremovable hard disk system. Storage capabilities in the 80 to 300 Megabyte range are common; the Gigabyte range is not far off for some networks. A tape cassette is a typically used medium for large size storage backups or backups done after hours. It is easy to use most tape system's software. If you are a systems administrator of a medium to large system, you need such a system to perform a back-up quickly and easily.

A tape backup unit also gives you greater flexibility. Most of the tape backup systems provide you with built-in storing of data selection criteria, either by the entire drive, a specified directory, specified files, or backing up files with modified-only status. Most tape systems software is menu driven, which makes the system easy to use and set up. Make sure to select a system that is compatible with NetWare and has the capability of backing up the hidden system files NET$BIND.SYS and NET$BVAL.SYS.

Many tape backup units on the market today range in price from $800 for a 40MB tape capacity to $7,000 for a 2.2 GB capacity.

Backing up with tape is much simpler and makes it easy to control and manage the storage of the backup. You will usually need only one tape per day for your backup, regardless of the total amount of space your file server has. The proper tape size depends on the capacity of the tape drive unit, the amount of space on your hard disk, and whether or not you are doing a full, partial, or modified file backup.

A tape backup system is unlike disk media in that it can be run stand-alone with a utility program that waits until a specific time to log on, start the backup, and then log out automatically after the backup is completed. This makes backing up during off-peak times more convenient.

For example, the Mountain Tape unit comes with a handy program called AUTORUN. This program allows you to specify commands you want automatically carried out on specific days at particular times. Type AUTORUN at the system prompt and the program lets you select the days of the week you want the tape backup unit to start. Then you have the opportunity of selecting whether you would like to select certain files for backup or directories. The commands you enter in the AUTORUN program are very clearly explained, and examples are given in the manual. It is very easy to use and set up. Once the AUTORUN program is set, all you have to do is start the program each day. After the backup has been run, you remove the tapes and store them.

You may also use this tape backup unit in manual mode and go through the simple menu system to select the files or directories you would like to back up. To restore files, you need to go through the manual menu mode, as restoring is an interactive procedure unless you are going to do a complete system restore.

Changing File Servers

Purpose: To access another file server or identify other file servers on the network.

Using SYSCON

TYPE/PRESS	RESULT:
SYSCON [Enter]	Displays SYSCON menu
C [Enter]	Selects Change Current Server
select server name	
[Enter]	Selects a server you are logged into
or	
INS	Displays a list of file servers
[Enter]	Selects new file server to log into
login name [Enter]	Specifies login name
password [Enter]	Specifies password

Using FCONSOLE

TYPE/PRESS	RESULT:
FCONSOLE [Enter]	Displays FCONSOLE menu
C [Enter]	Selects Change Current File Server
select server name	
[Enter]	Selects a server you are logged into
or	
INS	Displays a list of file servers
[Enter]	Selects new file server to log into
login name [Enter]	Specifies login name
password [Enter]	Specifies password

To log out from a file server, use the DEL key in either the FCONSOLE or SYSCON Change Current Server option.

Using SLIST

To display all servers you are logged into

```
SLIST [Enter]
```

Creating Groups

Purpose: To establish an organized entity for users that have common resource needs. SYSCON offers a method to create the group name and then mark each user to be added to the group. If you are adding multiple new users to a new or existing group, use MAKEUSER.

Using SYSCON

TYPE/PRESS	RESULT:
SYSCON [Enter]	Displays the SYSCON menu
G [Enter]	Selects Group Information menu
INS	Creates a New Group Name box
new group name [Enter]	Creates a new group
highlight the new group name	Selects the group
[Enter]	Displays the Group Information menu
highlight Full Name	
[Enter]	Displays a box to enter the full name
full group name [Enter]	Enters a longer full name description to the new group
Esc twice	Returns you to the main SYSCON menu

To delete a group, highlight the group name and press <DEL>.

To add a user or users to the new group from the SYSCON menu

TYPE/PRESS	RESULT:
G [Enter]	Selects Group Information menu
[Enter]	Completes the command
highlight the new group name	Selects the group
[Enter]	Displays the Group Information menu
highlight Member List	
[Enter]	Displays a list of users in the group (since this is a new group, none appear)
<INS>	Displays a list of all users created

highlight a user name to add [Enter]	Adds the user to the group
<ESC> twice	Returns you to the main SYSCON menu

Hint: To add multiple users to a group, at the Member List prompt press the F1 (Help) key on your machine to find the Mark key for your machine. Move the selection bar highlight to each name and press <Mark>. Press [Enter] when you have marked the last user to add to complete the command.

To delete a user from the group, repeat this process and press the <DEL> key on the user name to delete in place of the <INS> key step.

Using MAKEUSER

TYPE/PRESS	RESULT:
MAKEUSER [Enter]	Displays MAKEUSER main menu
[Enter]	Selects Create New USR file option
enter the following keywords: #GROUPS group1[;groupN]	Creates new group1 to groupN
Esc	Completes entry of keywords
Y [Enter]	Confirms completion of entry
filename [Enter]	Specifies filename as .USR file

To process the .USR file from DOS

```
MAKEUSER filename.USR [Enter]
```

NetWare will process the commands and create the new user based on the information you have entered. This method is useful when adding multiple new groups to the system. You still need to use SYSCON however, to assign existing users to new groups created with MAKEUSER.

Deleting Users

Purpose: To delete a user name from the system. SYSCON offers an easy method to delete one or more users.

Using SYSCON

TYPE/PRESS	RESULT:
SYSCON [Enter]	Displays the SYSCON main menu
U [Enter]	Selects User Information menu
highlights user name	Specifies a user name
MARK key	Selects the user for deletion
DEL	Displays Delete All Marked Users box
Y [Enter]	Deletes the users
Esc	Displays SYSCON main menu
Esc	Displays Exit menu
Y [Enter]	Confirms exit from SYSCON

Using MAKEUSER

TYPE/PRESS	RESULT:
MAKEUSER [Enter]	Displays MAKEUSER main menu
[Enter]	Selects Create New USR file option
enter the following keywords:	
#HOME_DIRECTORY	
directory path	Indicates the directory path for the HOME directories of the users to be deleted
#DELETE user1[,userN]	
	Deletes user1 and userN
Esc	Completes entry of keywords
Y [Enter]	Confirms completion of entry
filename [Enter]	Specifies filename as .USR file

To process the .USR file from DOS

```
MAKEUSER filename.USR [Enter]
```

NetWare will process the commands and create the new user based on the information you have entered. This method is useful when deleting several user names.

Directory Management

Purpose: To manage the file server directory structure and file attributes in order to assure organization, efficiency, and security.

Using FLAG

Purpose: Changes DOS file attributes for a file or group of files using flags:

N Normal

S Shareable

NS Nonsharable

RW Read/Write

RO Read/Only

I Indexes large files

T Flags transactional for TTS

Program files should be flagged S and RO to protect users from writing over them.

To display DOS file attributes for a file(s), type

```
FLAG filename [Enter]
```

To change DOS file attributes for a file(s), type

```
FLAG filename flag(s) [Enter]
```

To change all .EXE files to RO, type

```
FLAG *.EXE RO [Enter]
```

See also "Using FILER" in this section.

Using LISTDIR

Purpose: Views the directory structure of a volume, drive, or directory. Also views maximum rights mask (directory rights) and date and time of creation for each directory below the specified directory. Flag options are:

/R Displays rights mask

/D Displays creation date and time

/S Displays all subdirectories below first level

/A Displays all available information for each specified directory (equal to /R/S/A used together).

To view the entire directory structure of the volume SYS, type

```
LISTDIR SYS: /S [Enter]
```

To view the entire directory structure of a drive, type

```
LISTDIR G: /S [Enter]
```

See also "Using FILER" for changing directory creation date and time, owner, or rights mask.

Using NCOPY

Purpose: Copies files from one location to another. Similar to DOS COPY command, but faster when copying between file server directories. Note that the separator TO is used (but not required), unlike DOS COPY (space only).

To copy files using NCOPY from one location to another

```
NCOPY [directory path/]filename TO [directory path/]filename
[Enter]
```

Using NDIR

Purpose: Searches for a file in a server directory path(s).

To search for a file in any subdirectory on the SYS volume, type

```
NDIR sys:filename subdirectory [Enter]
```

Note: If you type sys in lower or upper case, subdirectory name must also be typed in the same case.

Using RENDIR

Purpose: Renames an existing directory to a new name. Eliminates having to copy files to a new directory just to change the name.

To rename one directory to another name, type

```
RENDIR [directory path] old name TO [directory path] new name [Enter]
```

Using PURGE

Purpose: Permanently removes files marked for deletion from the file server that have not been overwritten by new files.

To purge files from a directory, type

```
PURGE [Enter]
```

Only files that were deleted using DEL or ERASE are removed.

Using SALVAGE

Purpose: Recovers file(s) deleted using the last DEL or ERASE command that have not been purged from the system or overwritten by new files.

To recover files from a directory, type

```
SALVAGE [Enter]
```

Files that were deleted using the last DEL or ERASE commmand are restored.

Using FILER

Purpose: Manages a server or workstation directory structure by allowing the supervisor to change a directory or subdirectory creation date, time, or owner; a file creation date, last accessed or modified date, or owner; or assign the "Execute Only" file attribute. Available to Version 2.1 and above users only.

Figure 4.5 FILER main menu.

To change a directory's data, from that directory

TYPE/PRESS	RESULT:
filer [Enter]	Displays the Filer main menu
C [Enter]	Selects the Current Directory Info option
C [Enter]	Selects the Creation Date option

erase the date using the Backspace key	Cancels old creation date
mm-dd-yy or mm/dd/yy [Enter]	Enters new creation date; displays creation time entry box
erase the time using the Backspace key	Cancels old creation time
hh:mm [Enter]	Enters new creation time
O [Enter]	Selects the Owner option
Ins [Enter]	Displays a list of users to select new owner from
Esc	Displays the Filer main menu
Esc	Exits the Filer menu

To change a subdirectory's data, from that subdirectory:

TYPE/PRESS	RESULT:
filer [Enter]	Displays the Filer main menu
S [Enter]	Selects the Subdirectory Info option
subdirectory [Enter] or mark each subdirectory name to change with the Mark key [Enter]	Selects subdirectory name(s) to change
C [Enter]	Selects the Creation Date option
erase the date using the Backspace key	Cancels old creation date
mm-dd-yy or mm/dd/yy [Enter]	Enters new creation date; displays creation time entry box
erase the time using the Backspace key	Cancels old creation time

hh:mm	
[Enter]	Enters new creation time
O [Enter]	Selects the Owner option
Ins	Displays a list of users to select new owner from
[Enter]	Completes the command
Esc	Displays the Filer main menu
Esc	Exits the Filer menu

To change a file's data, from that subdirectory

TYPE/PRESS	RESULT:
filer [Enter]	Displays the Filer main menu
F [Enter]	Selects the File Info option
highlight the filename	
[Enter]	Selects the file to change
C [Enter]	Selects the Creation Date option
erase the date using the Backspace key	Cancels old creation date
mm-dd-yy or mm/dd/yy	
[Enter]	Enters new creation date; displays creation time entry box
erase the time using the Backspace key	Cancels old creation time
hh:mm	
[Enter]	Enters new creation time
O [Enter]	Selects the Owner option
Ins	Displays a list of users to select new owner from
[Enter]	Completes the command
Esc	Displays the Filer main menu
Esc	Exits the Filer menu

Attributes or settings that affect access to a file can also be changed or flagged using either the FLAG command or the FILER menu (for most attributes) as long as you have a Modify right to a file. See "Using FLAG" previously described in this section. See "Trustee

Rights" for more on setting rights. Attributes that can be changed include:

1. **Execute Only:** Prevents files with a .COM or .EXE extension from being copied, deleted, or modified. Once a file is flagged with this attribute, it can not be reflagged to remove the attribute.
2. **Read Only:** Allows users to read a file but denies writing to it.
3. **Read/Write:** Allows users to read or write to a file.
4. **Shareable:** Allows users to share or use the same file at the same time.
5. **Nonshareable:** Allows only one user to use a file at one time.
6. **Normal:** Sets the attributes for a file to Nonshareable and Read/Write. Can be flagged only from DOS.
7. **Hidden:** Hides a file from a directory search. Is set using the HIDEFILE command. See "Using HIDEFILE" for more on effects of setting a file's attribute to Hidden.
8. **Indexed:** Re-indexes the File Allocation Table (FAT) to allow the read/write head to efficiently access the information needed to retrieve larger files faster.
9. **Modified Since Last Backup:** Set after a file has been modifed after a backup.
10. **System:** Set for files that are used for the system to function; hides files from a directory search. HIDEFILE sets this flag on; SHOWFILE sets this flag off.
11. **Transactional:** Sets files to be protected by SFT's Transaction Tracking feature. Ensures that when a file is modified, either all changes are made or no changes are made and prevents data corruption. Used only on data files.

To change a file's* attribute *data, from the subdirectory with the files to change

TYPE/PRESS	RESULT:
filer [Enter]	Displays the Filer main menu
F [Enter]	Selects the File Information option
highlight the filename [Enter]	Selects the file to change
A [Enter]	Selects the Attributes option; displays a list of attributes attached to the file

To delete attributes

Mark each attribute to delete using the Mark key	Selects the attributes to delete
DEL	Displays Remove File Attribute box
Y [Enter]	Deletes attribute(s)

To add attributes

INS	Displays the Other File Attributes list
Mark each attribute to add using the Mark key	Selects the attributes to add
[Enter]	Adds all marked attributes to the file

To quit either deletion or insertion of attributes

Esc	Displays the File Information menu
Esc	Displays the Files menu
Esc	Displays the Filer main menu
Esc	Exits the Filer menu
Y [Enter]	Confirms exit

Using HIDEFILE: Hiding a File From a Directory

Purpose: Hides a file or group of files from a directory display by setting the Hidden and System DOS attributes. Files hidden do not show after issuing a DIR command, cannot be copied over using COPY filename, hidden filename or copied to another directory, or deleted using the DEL or ERASE command. Files can be displayed using the TYPE command, accessed by many other DOS commands and can be modified. NetWare utilities BACKUP and RESTORE can access hidden files.

To hide a file or group of files from the SYS:SYSTEM directory, type

```
HIDEFILE [drive:] [directory] filename [Enter]
```

The screen will display a message after hiding the file such as:

```
fileserver/SYS:SYSTEM
filename hidden
```

Hint: You can use DOS wildcard symbols * and ? to specify multiple files.

To cancel a HIDEFILE command, use the SHOWFILE command.

Using SHOWFILE: Displaying a File From a Directory

Purpose: Resets the status of DOS attributes System and Hidden to one or more files that have been hidden using the HIDEFILE command. Allows the DIR command to display the filename(s).

To show a file or group of files from the SYS:SYSTEM directory, type

```
SHOWFILE [drive:] [directory] filename [Enter]
```

Hint: You can use DOS wildcard symbols * and ? to specify multiple files.

Using HOLDON: Keeping a File Open to Prevent Changes

Purpose: Holds open or allows exclusive access to all files accessed during an application work session. Denies all other users access who have rights to files during the application session. Prevents a file from being printed. Useful for a single-user application who does not have the capability to handle two or more users making changes to a file at the same time. Most of these programs allow each user access, but changes made by the first user who has completed and saved a file are overwritten by any other user who completes and saves the same file. This command prevents this from happening.

Prior to issuing the applications program execution command, type

```
HOLDON [Enter]
```

To cancel the HOLDON command, issue the HOLDOFF command after exiting the application or by running an application's DOS shell (temporary exit to DOS).

Using HOLDOFF: Setting Applications Data Files to Allow Changes or Printing

Purpose: Reverses the effect of the HOLDON utility command by clearing the open status of the files and allowing other users to access the files during an application session. After exiting applications programs, the files that were opened are closed automatically regardless of whether the HOLDON command was issued.

After exiting or issuing a temporary exit from an applications program, type

```
HOLDOFF [Enter]
```

You can return to the applications program and print or allow another user access to one or more files.

Documenting the System

Purpose: To identify file servers on a network, topology, hardware, and software installed at each file server and workstation, network printers, vendor support list, file server directory structure, system login script components, groups and users, and rights.

(See "Identifying and Documenting Servers and Topology" in Chapter 2.)

Electronic Mail Programs

Purpose: Allows users to electronically create, send, or read memos for and from other network users. May also allow file transfers, password protection, creation of user groups, or other features depending on which mail program is used.

Using Novell MAIL

Purpose: Allows users to electronically create, send, or read memos for and from other network users. Only available in NetWare Version 2.0x.

To create a memo

TYPE/PRESS	RESULT:
mail [Enter]	Loads the EMS (Electronic Mail Service) program; displays a > prompt
EDIT name [Enter]	Prompts you for a "subject" or title
subject [Enter]	Enters the subject for the memo
type the memo [Enter]	Enters the memo text into the file
F2	Completes the memo entry; displays the >prompt

To send a memo from the > prompt

TYPE/PRESS	RESULT:
SEND name TO user or group name [Enter]	Sends the memo NAME to a user or group

To read a memo from the > prompt

TYPE/PRESS	RESULT:
CHECK [Enter]	Looks for any mail
READ MAIL [Enter]	Lists any mail
highlight name F2	Selects mail to read

Place First Class
Postage Here
Post Office
Will Not Deliver
Without Postage

Brady Books
15 Columbus Circle
New York, NY 10023

ATT: J. Padlad

To quit mail from the >prompt

TYPE/PRESS	RESULT:
QUIT [Enter]	Quits the > prompt and returns to DOS

For more on using Novell mail, see the User Manual.

Table 4.1 Electronic Mail Features

● Yes ○ No

◒ Deficient

▼ Limited only by available disk space

Messaging options	DaVinci	Network Courier	ccMail	Higgins Mail	Transcend
Maximum file attachments	▼	100	20	26	▼
Pop-up alarm TSR (RAM used)	2K	12K	11K	3K	○
Messaging TSR (RAM used)	100K	78K	77K	○	172K
Unload TSRs from memory	○[1]	●	●	○	○
Carbon copies	●	●	●	●	●
Blind carbon copies	●	○	●	○	○
Return receipt	●	●	●	●	●
Private mail lists	●	●	●	●	●
Public mail lists	●	●	●	●	○
Priority classifications	●	●	○	●	●
Password by message	●	○	○	○	○
See message while replying	●	○	○	○	○
Phone message from	●	●[2]	○	●	○
Bulletin boards	○	●	●	○	○
Message management					
Stores mail in folders	○	●	●	○	●
Saves copies of outgoing mail	●	●	○	●	●
Saves drafts	●	○	○	●	●
Global processing of mail	●	●	◒[3]	○	●
Sorts by sender, subject, priority	○	●	○	○	○
Displays by					
sender	●	○	●	○	○
subject	●	○	●	◒[4]	○
date range	●	○	●	◒[4]	○
text	○	●	○	○	○
priority	●	○	○	○	○

Text editing	DaVinci	Network Courier	ccMail	Higgins Mail	Transcend
Imports / exports ASCII files	●	●	●	◒[5]	●
Block move and delete	●	○	●	○	●
True word wrap[6]	●	○	○	○	●
Cuts and pastes from ASCII files	○	●	◒[7]	○	○
Search and replace	○	○	●	○	○
Set text attributes	○	○	●	○	○
Snapshot utility	○	○	●	○	○
Graphics utility	○	○	●	○	○
Connectivity					
Remote PC access	●[8]	○[8,9]	●[8]	●[8]	●[8]
InterLAN routing	●	●[8]	●[8]	●[8]	○
MHS compatibility	●	○	●[8]	○	●
Fax	●[10]	○	●[10]	●[8]	●[10]
On-Line E-mail services					
Easylink	●[10]	○	●[8]	○	○
Telemail	●[10]	○	●[8]	○	●[10]
Dialcom	○	○	○	○	●[11]
MCI Mail	●[10]	○[9]	○[10]	○	●[10]
Mainframe / mini gateways	●[10]	○[9]	●[8]	○[8]	●[10]

[1]Leaves 13K "dispatcher" resident.

[2]Free third-party utility available.

[3]You can globally tag attachments only when sending, not receiving.

[4]You must assign subject keyword manually on receiving end.

[5]Imports only.

[6]Distinguishes between hard and soft returns.

[7]You must input range of line numbers from undisplayed file.

[8]Extra-cast option.

[9]Not available at press time.

[10]Requires extra-cost, MHS-compatible third-party option.

[11]Via local modem, no group gateway.

Using Other Mail Programs

Purpose: Allows users to electronically create, send, or read memos for and from other network users. Available for NetWare Versions 2.1 and above.

Table 4.1 shows a features comparison of five electronic mail programs that work with NetWare Version 2.1 (some also support 2.0a):.

The following is a list of the name, version, company, address, telephone, prices, accessories, requirements, and technical support information for the electronic mail systems in Table 4.1.

Table 4.2 Electronic Mail Program Information

Product: cc:Mail 3.03
Company: cc:Mail, Inc.
Address: 385 Sherman Ave.
Palo Alto, CA 94306
Telephone: (415) 321-0430
Price: 25 users, $695
125 users, $290
Accessories: OS/2 Version $495
remote access: 1–9 users, $295/user
10–24 users, $195/user
25–99 users, $150/user
Gateway (includes MHS): $1,295
Import/Export API: $995
PROFS: $2,200
EasyLink: $695
Telemail: $695
Requirements: 320K, DOS 3.1 +
Technical Support: 90 days free, then $200 per year; toll-free number, M–F 7–7

Product: DaVinci eMail for DOS 1.0
Company: DaVinci Systems
Address: P.O. Box 5427
Raleigh, NC 27650
Telephone: 919-839-2000
Price: 5 users, $295: server, $995
Accessories: single user (remote), $150;
single user MHS (remote), $100; DaVinci for Windows, $1,145 per server; Windows/DOS Version $1,495 per server; UNIX gateway, $995; gateways for fax, MCI Mail, SNADS, All-in-1, and other systems available for MHS via third parties.
Requirements: 384K, DOS 3.0 or later version, hard disk recommended.
Technical Support: M-F 8:30 a.m. to 9.p.m.

(continued)

Table 4.2 (continued)

Product: Higgins Mail 2.2
Company: Enable Software/Higgins Group
Address: Northway 10, Executive Park
Ballston Lake, NY 12019
Telephone: 800/888-0684
518/877-8600
Price: 20 users, $495
Accessories: Higgins Remote, $395 per user; Higgins Exchange (required for interLAN routing and following options), $1,595; PROFS, $995; Fax link, $995 (requires fax board); 3+Mail gateway, $495; SNADS, $5,000 and up; API, $995.
Requirements: 640K, hard disk, DOS 3.1 or later version.
Technical Support: toll-free number, M-F 7 a.m. to 5 p.m.

Product: The Network Courier 2.0
Company: Consumers Software
Address: 73 Water St., 7th Floor
Vancouver, BC
V6B 1A1 Canada
Telephone: 800/663-8935
604/688-4548
Price: 6 users, $295; 100 users, $695; 500 users, $2495.
Accessories: Windows/DOS upgrade, $595; interLAND Version (required for following options), $995 (150 users). Following options unavailable at press time: Modem Mail, $495 per server, $95 per remote PC; MCI Mail, $695; SNADS, $2,500 per server, $1,000 per post office; PROFS, $5,000 per host, $1,000 per post office
Requirements: 256K, hard disk, DOS 3.1 or later version
Technical Support: no toll-free number, M-F 9 a.m. to 5 p.m.

Product: Transend PC Complete 4.1
Company: Transend Corp.
Address: 884 Portola Rd.
Portola Valley, CA 94025
Telephone: 415/851-3402
Price:

Number of users	Price per PC
1–9	$229
10–24	$199
25-99	$185
100-199	$175
200-499	$165
500 +	$150

LAN E-mail-only version $295 for 5 users.
Accessories: same third-party MHS options as DaVinci, except remote modem access requires MHS ($100) plus copy of Transend at each remote site.
Requirements: 320K, Novell NetWare 2.0 or later version, MHS, DOS 2.0 or later version.
Technical Support: no toll-free number, M-F 8 a.m. to 5 p.m.

Installing/Loading Applications Software

Purpose: To add an applications software program to the file server in order to allow users to share program or data files.

To add a program to the server

1. Review the hardware requirements: disk space needed, minimum RAM memory, display or printer models supported. Ensure that you have the proper type of hardware and that the recommended video display monitors and memory adaptors do not conflict with the network interface card in your workstations. Call the manufacturer of the applications program if you are unsure of its compatibility with network cards before making a purchase decision.
2. Determine if a special network version is included with the program or if it's available. Review any special considerations documented in the manual.
3. Log into the network as a supervisor. Make a new subdirectory to store the program files using the MD DOS command or other program utility. Create any other subdirectories that users need to share data files related to the new applications program.
4. Copy the program files to the new directory. Install the program using its install program if necessary. Copy any data files needed to the new directory(s).
5. Determine which users need access to the program. If it is a logical group, for example, a word processing department, update that group's trustee assignments or create a new group using the SYSCON menu utility. Update the trustee rights of each individual user who will need access to the program.
6. Edit the system login script or each user's login script to include a search or logical drive mapping to the new program directory. Remember, you can use the Paste feature to copy login script lines between login scripts. (See "Login Scripts" for details). Save the changes for each user.
7. Test the system login script or each revised user's login to ensure that the proper access is established. You should load the new pro-

gram, create a new file, access an existing file, and print a file from each network printer available to the logged in user.

8. Update any system menus that should display the new applications program as a choice.
9. Include the new data files and program files in the routine backup procedure.
10. Reconfigure any printer requirements (i.e., laser printer or other special *driver* sets or special sets of printer codes for network or local printers), display requirements (i.e. workstation graphics display type, select colors for workstation display) or the data file default storage directory (i.e., network drive or local workstation drive) for each workstation.

Intruder Detection

(See "Login Restrictions.")

Logging Into the Network

Purpose: Accesses network's resources based on custom assignments via a user name and password. The workstation you want to log into should be attached to the network by loading the network shell commands. See "Shells" for more information on loading the shell.

Using LOGIN

Purpose: Permits a user access to the network.

To log into a network, type

```
LOGIN username [Enter]
```

Note: Once logged in, you can log into the network as a new user by repeating the command without using the LOGOUT command. Logging into the network as a new user logs out the previous user.

Using LOGOUT

Purpose: Ends a user's work session on the network.

To log out of a network, type

```
LOGOUT [Enter]
```

Using SYSTIME

Purpose: Sets the workstation clock to the time of the file server.

To set the workstation clock after logging in, type

```
SYSTIME [Enter]
```

This command can be added to a login script using #SYSTIME (See the section "Login Scripts").

Using USERLIST

Purpose: Displays a list of active user names, login date and times, or network and node address (using /a option) on screen.

To display the user list, type

```
USERLIST [server/name] [user] [/a] [Enter]
```

Note: If you type USERLIST [username]CR, the command will confirm whether the user name is logged into the current file server with the name, date, and time of login or a message informing you that they are not logged in.

Using FCONSOLE Connection

Purpose: To display a list of one or more users connected on the current file server. The list is updated every two seconds. Supervisors or users with supervisor equivalence can perform tasks such as:

Broadcast messages.

Clear connections.

View status of logical record locks.

View status of open files/physical records.

Examine semaphores.

View usage statistics.

For more on using these tasks, see the NetWare *Supervisor Reference Manual.*

To display a list of connected users

TYPE/PRESS	RESULT:
FCONSOLE [Enter]	Displays the FCONSOLE main menu
C [Enter]	Selects Connection Information

A list of users and their current connections appears as shown below.

Current Connections

User name 1
User name 4
User name 7

Using WHOAMI

Purpose: Displays your user name, file server(s) you are attached to, your connection number, and the date and time of your last login. Options include:

/G Displays groups you are a member of

/S Displays your security equivalences

/R Displays your effective rights in the network

/A Displays information for /G,/S, and /R option

To identify the user name after logged in, type

```
WHOAMI [Enter]
```

To identify your groups after logged in, type

```
WHOAMI /G [Enter]
```

Login Scripts

Purpose: Stores a file with a set of customized commands that perform tasks when a user logs into the network. Commands can use variables that tell NetWare information about the user logging in, such as user ID name or group membership, as well as the environment, such as the time, day of week, or workstation ID. There are three types of login scripts: the default, system, and individual. The default login script comes built into the system and cannot be changed. However, it is disabled once an individual login script is created for a user. The system login script performs its tasks first for each user who logs into the system. The individual login script is then executed and may be designed to meet each user's specific needs.

Login scripts can do tasks such as: logical drive or search directory mappings, changing the current drive, running a program, testing for conditions with IF statements, or displaying messages. Login scripts are created or modified using the SYSCON menu.

The systems administrator should not have to modify the system login script, which is typically set up by the person who installed your network. It is, however, a great place for the systems administrator to set up drive mappings for groups or other group dependent options. You will see examples of a systems login script that directs NetWare to do certain tasks, depending on whether a user is a member of a specific task area. In general, the systems administrator's tasks can include copying or creating an individual login script for new users.

There are several commands that can be used in a login script. They are each described in detail below. A section describing variables that can be used in commands follows.

Using Commands within in Scripts

ATTACH

Used to attach (or connect) to another file server in your internetwork system. This command is only used on systems that have more than one file server.

```
ATTACH file server name
```

BREAK ON

Used to stop the execution of your login script during the login process. If you have entered the BREAK ON command in your login script, you can press CTRL/C or CTRL/BREAK at any time to abort the normal execution of your login script. The default form is BREAK OFF. We recommend leaving it set to the default unless you want users to be able to stop the login script and interrupt drive mappings or other valuable commands. Below is an example of using the command to allow the user to stop the login procedure.

```
BREAK ON
```

COMSPEC

Used to specify the operating system directory that DOS uses to reload the command processor file COMMAND.COM. This command is especially useful when your network is using multiple versions of DOS. If more than one version of DOS is available on your network, an operating system directory is created for each DOS version. The COMSPEC command will automatically select and reload the proper COMMAND.COM (the command interpreter file) for the computer and operating system you are using. You usually find this command in your system login script set up by the installer. Should you install another version of DOS on your system, you will need to change or modify the way it is set.

To use the command set the COMSPEC equal to a search drive and the filename COMMAND.COM as follows:

```
COMSPEC=S2COMMAND.COM
```

DISPLAY AND FDISPLAY

Used to display the contents of a specified text file on a workstation screen during the login process.

To display all text entered into the file SYSNEWS.TXT, type

```
FDISPLAY SYSPUBLIC/MESSAGES/SYSNEWS.TXT
```

DISPLAY works similarly, but it displays the full file, including nontext characters.

DOS BREAK

Used to control whether any programs or DOS commands can be interrupted with CTRL/BREAK after you have logged in (Note: this command does not replace the login script BREAK command). With DOS BREAK ON in your login script, if you press CTRL/BREAK, the program or DOS command will be interrupted only after the login procedure has been completely executed. This helps in preventing unexpected termination of the login procedure. DOS BREAK OFF is the system default form.

DOS SET

Used in your login script to set a variable in a DOS environment to a specfied value. It is identical to the DOS SET command except it requires you to place double quotation marks (" ") around values, while the DOS SET command does not. Variables that can be set include: PROMPT, USR, and others that are set with the DOS SET command at the command line (refer to the DOS manual for more on DOS SET).

To set the DOS prompt to the directory path name, type

```
SET PROMPT=''$P$G''
```

DOS VERIFY

Note: If this command is used in the AUTOEXEC.BAT file this is unnecessary in the login script.

Used to verify whether or not data copied to a local drive has been copied correctly. The DOS COPY command, unlike the NetWare copy command (NCOPY), does not automatically verify that data has been copied to a local drive. If you want DOS to make the same verification, you must enter the DOS VERIFY ON command in your login script.

DRIVE

Used to specify as a default drive a drive other than the first network drive. If a user uses an application located on a specific drive more often than others, for example word processing, you can alter the login script to make the directory current after login. Unless you have entered this command in a login script, the default drive is set to the first network drive, which is often initially assigned to the home directory where it was logged in.

For example, to make drive G current after login, type

```
DRIVE G:
```

EXIT

Used to terminate execution of the LOGIN command line utility. The command is used in the login script command to execute .COM, .EXE, .BAT files, and DOS internal commands, such as DIR.

For example, to execute a SETUP.BAT batch file used to activate menus or other programs, type

```
EXIT "SETUP.BAT"
```

EXTERNAL PROGRAM EXECUTION (#)

Used to execute a command that is external to the login script, such as .EXE and .COM program files. This command should appear *after* MAP assignments since the program executes in the environment of drive mappings, default drives, and search drives set up previously in the login script.

Warning: Do not use # or EXIT commands in your login scripts to start terminate and stay resident (TSR) programs such as SideKick or terminal emulators. Instead, include a command to load these types of programs in a .BAT file and execute the .BAT file using the EXIT command.

FIRE PHASERS

Used to generate a sound like a phaser gun fired by space heroes. It alerts the user that certain conditions exist.

The following example alerts users that they have mail

```
IF NEW_MAIL = "YES" THEN FIRE PHASERS 3 TIMES
```

IF. . . . .THEN

Used to make the login process perform commands conditionally, depending on whether specified conditions are true.

To display a message that there is no mail for a user, first check to see whether there is mail by examining the variable NEW_MAIL and writing a message on the screen using IF THEN as follows:

```
IF NEW_MAIL="NO" THEN WRITE "NO MAIL FOR YOU TODAY,"; LOGIN_NAME
```

Each of the following two examples checks to see if there is mail and takes an appropriate action, either loads the mail program or fires phasers:

```
IF NEW_MAIL="YES" THEN EXIT "MAIL"

IF NEW_MAIL = "YES" THEN FIRE PHASERS 3 TIMES
```

To check to see if a user is a member of a certain group, use the variable MEMBER OF as follows:

```
IF MEMBER OF "ACCOUNTING" THEN INCLUDE SYS:PUBLIC/SYSNEWS
```

To display a friendly message using the DAY_OF_WEEK variable and the WRITE command:

```
IF DAY_OF_WEEK = "WEDNESDAY" THEN WRITE "AWRIGHT, IT'S HUMP
DAY!!"
```

INCLUDE

Causes the login script to process "subscripts" that are not contained in the login script currently being processed. These subscripts are simply text files that contain valid script commands (any command explained in Chapter 4 of this book). Subscripts can be created and edited using any text editor or word processor.

Note: The INCLUDE command does not function in the same way as the DISPLAY or FDISPLAY commands. In order for it to display text as shown in this example, the included file must contain WRITE commands.

MACHINE NAME

Used to set the machine name of the station to the specified name. This command is necessary for some programs written to run under PC DOS.

MAP

Sets drive mappings and search drive mappings for all network users. Drive mappings in the login script will be in effect each time the user logs in to the file server. This command enables you as the systems administrator to set the system and application programs to run transparently. As you add new applications programs to the system you will use this command. See "Mapping Logical Drives and Search Directories" for more on mapping. You can turn the display of mapped drives off with the MAP DISPLAY OFF command. The NetWare default is to show them on screen, which can be intimidating for some users.

To map search or logical drives in a login script with MAP, type

```
MAP DISPLAY OFF
MAP S1:=SYS:PUBLIC
MAP S2:=SYS:PUBLIC\%MACHINE\%OS\%OS_VERSION
MAP S3:=SYS:ACCOUNTING
MAP F:=SYS:
MAP H:=SYS:DATABASE
MAP I:=SYS:WORDPROCESSING
MAP J:=SYS:SPREADSHEET
MAP G:=SYS:HOME\%LOGIN-NAME
```

PAUSE

Used to make the execution of the login script pause and give you a message on screen "Strike a key when ready . . . ." This command is useful if you want the user to be able to read what is on the screen.

PCCOMPATIBLE

Used to include a filename with the "EXIT" login script command on all computers that are IBM PC compatible; you can also use it with computers that are not 100 percent IBM PC compatible. If the machine name in your SHELL.CFG file is set to another name (for example, COMPAQ), to access a different version of DOS, you must use the PCCOMPATIBLE (or COMPATIBLE) login script command to inform the login program that your machine is IBM PC compatible.

For example, if you are working on an IBM PC compatible and you want to exit to SYSCON from within your login script, on a blank line, type

```
PCCOMPATIBLE
EXIT SYSCON
```

REMARK

Used as REMARK, REM, *, or ; to insert explanatory text into your login script. Any text following those commands will be ignored when the LOGIN command interprets and executes your login script. The "remark" will not appear on your screen. This is helpful in documenting your system or user login script commands. Including explanatory text will make your login script much easier for you to read and understand.

```
REM This is a reminder that SYSACCTG maps to M
```

WRITE

Used to create customized login messages. You can enter a single command or include a list of text strings or identifiers separated by semincolons (;) after any WRITE command. Each message will appear on a new line on your screen, unless you place a semicolon at the end of the WRITE command line. Multiple WRITE commands will generate a one-line display. Text strings must be enclosed in double quotation marks and can include the following super-characters:

\ r for a carriage return

\ n for a new line

\ for an embedded quotation mark

\ 7 to sound a beep

When the WRITE command is executed, a variable can be used to display its contents as text and then displayed on your workstation screen, but the variable must be in upper case characters and preceded by the percent symbol.

To use WRITE to display a text message, type

```
WRITE "CHECKING FOR MAIL"
```

WRITE can mix text and variables:

```
WRITE "GOOD %GREETING_TIME, %LOGIN_NAME
```

WRITE can be based on a conditional IF command that checks variables:

```
IF NEW_MAIL="NO" THEN WRITE "NO MAIL FOR YOU TODAY,"; LOGIN_NAME

IF DAY OF WEEK = "WEDNESDAY" THEN WRITE "AWRIGHT IT'S HUMP DAY!!"
```

Using Variables in Login Scripts

The following variables or *identifiers* represent text information. They can be used with the IF...THEN command as well as the WRITE command. They can also be used with commands for which you specify a path name such as COMSPEC.

Table 4.3 IDENTIFIERS

IDENTIFIER	SCREEN DISPLAY
HOUR	Hour of day or night (1-12)
HOUR24	Hour (00–23)
MINUTE	Minute (00–59)
SECOND	Second (00–59)

AM_PM	Day or night (am or pm)
MONTH	Month number (01–12)
MONTH_NAME	Month name (January, June, etc.)
DAY	Day number (01–31)
NDAY_OF_WEEK	Weekday number (1–7, Sunday's 1)
YEAR	Year in full format (1989, 2001)
SHORT_YEAR	Year in short form (89, 01, etc.)
DAY_OF_WEEK	Day of week (Monday, Friday, etc.)
LOGIN_NAME	User's unique login name
FULL_NAME	User's full name (from SYSCON full filename)
STATION	Workstation number
P_STATION	Physical station (12 hex digits)
GREETING_TIME	Morning, afternoon, or evening
SHELL_TYPE	Shell type number (0, 27, 3, etc.)
NEW_MAIL	YES or NO, indicating whether or not new mail has arrived. Your mailbox is checked automatically when you log in, and the correct value ("YES" or "NO") is assigned.
OS	The workstation's operating system, (MSDOS)
OS_VERSION	The version of the workstation's DOS, (V3.20)
MACHINE	The machine the shell was written for (IBM_PC)
SMACHINE	Short machine name (IBM)
ERROR_LEVEL	A value. For example, 0 (no errors) or any number other than 0 (errors)
MEMBER_OF_GROUPNAME	Name of group

The sample login script below gives you an idea of how the different commands might be used in your login scripts.

Listing 4.1 Sample login script

```
WRITE "GOOD %GREETING_TIME, %LOGIN_NAME

WRITE "CHECKING FOR MAIL"

IF NEW_MAIL="NO" THEN WRITE "NO MAIL FOR YOU TODAY,"; LOGIN_NAME

IF MEMBER OF "ACCOUNTING" THEN INCLUDE SYS:PUBLIC\ SYSNEWS

IF NEW_MAIL="YES"
 THEN BEGIN
```

```
  FIRE PHASERS 3 TIMES
  MAIL
 END
 EXIT

IF DAY_OF_WEEK = "WEDNESDAY" THEN WRITE "AWRIGHT, IT'S HUMP
DAY!!"

REMARK Be sure to check system mail
REM Update the SYSNEWS file!!

MAP DISPLAY OFF
MAP S1:=SYS:PUBLIC
MAP S2:=SYS:PUBLIC\%MACHINE\%OS\%OS_VERSION
COMSPEC=S2:COMMAND.COM
MAP S3:=SYS:ACCOUNTING
MAP F:=SYS:
MAP H:=SYS:DATABASE
MAP I:=SYS:WORDPROCESSING
MAP J:=SYS:SPREADSHEET
MAP G:=SYS:HOME\%LOGIN_NAME
DRIVE G:

FDISPLAY SYS:PUBLIC\MESSAGES\SYSNEWS.TXT
REM displays messages in SYSNEWS.TXT
SET PROMPT="$P$G"
DOS BREAK ON
DOS VERIFY ON
EXIT "SETUP.BAT"
REM "SETUP.BAT" CAN BE A BATCH FILE THAT A SYSTEMS ADMINISTRATOR
USES TO ACTIVATE MENUS OR OTHER PROGRAMS.

@ECHO OFF
REM Turns off display to screen
CAPTURE P=0 NB TI=5 NFF
REM Captures data to be printed to Print Queue, NB= No Banner will be
  printed, TI=Time before print queue will start printing, NFF= No
  form feed will be sent to printer after print job is finished.
MENU XYZ
REM Starts menu script XYZ
```

System Login Script Modification

To create or modify a system login script for version 2.1 and above using SYSCON

TYPE/PRESS	RESULT:
SYSCON [Enter]	Displays SYSCON menu
S [Enter]	Selects Supervisor Options
S [Enter]	Selects System Login Script
make any changes	
Esc	Exits the script and presents a confirmation box
Y [Enter]	Saves changes

To modify the SYSTEM login script for NetWare Version 2.0

TYPE/PRESS	RESULT:
SYSCON [Enter]	Brings up SYSCON menu
S	Selects System Login Script
[Enter]	Completes

To create or modify an individual user's script, use the following steps:

TYPE/PRESS	RESULT:
SYSCON [Enter]	
U [Enter]	Selects User Information
select user name [Enter]	
L [Enter]	Selects Login Script
make any changes	
Esc	Exits the script and presents a confirmation box
Y [Enter]	Saves changes

Hint: To copy another user's entire script, after you select Login Script, a box appears with the message: "The Login Script Does Not Exist." Backspace the name of the user listed, type the name of the user whose login script you want to copy, and press [Enter].

To copy part of one user's script to another:

TYPE/PRESS	RESULT:
SYSCON [Enter]	
U [Enter]	Selects User Information
select user name	

to copy FROM [Enter]	
L [Enter]	Selects Login Script
Mark the part of the script to copy with the Mark and arrow keys	Specifies the script to copy FROM
DEL	Deletes the marked text and copies it to the paste buffer
INS	Reinserts the deleted text and keeps it in paste buffer
Esc	Exits the script and presents a confirmation box
N [Enter]	Ignores changes
Esc	Returns to list of users
select user name to copy TO [Enter]	
L [Enter]	Selects Login Script
Move cursor to point to insert copied login script	Specifies the location to copy TO
INS	Copies paste buffer text

You can repeat this procedure for any number of users.

Login Restrictions

Purpose: To increase security of the file server by increasing the difficulty of access for unauthorized users.

NetWare 2.1 and above offers four types of restrictions:

1. **Account restrictions:** Disables the account, sets an expiration date, limits concurrent connections, allows the user to change the password, sets password requirement and length, sets password change dates, and limits disk space. Shown in Figure 4.6.

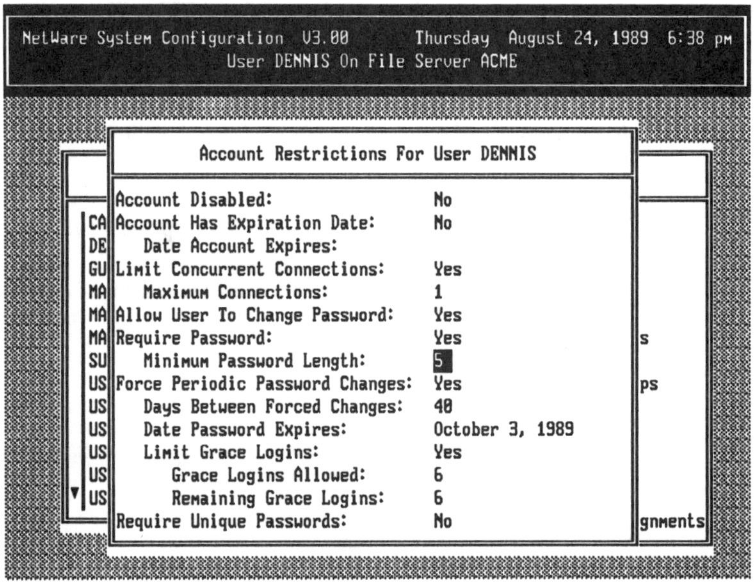

Figure 4.6 SYSCON Account Restriction display.

2. **Time restrictions:** Sets hours a user can log in. Shown in Figure 4.7.
3. **Station restrictions:** Sets physical workstation locations a user can use to log into the network. Set from one to all stations.
4. **Intruder detection:** Sets detection on or off, sets number of incorrect login attempts allowed, sets bad login retention or waiting-period time in minutes, hours, or days. Sets lock status after detection period in minutes, hours, or days. Shown in Figure 4.8.

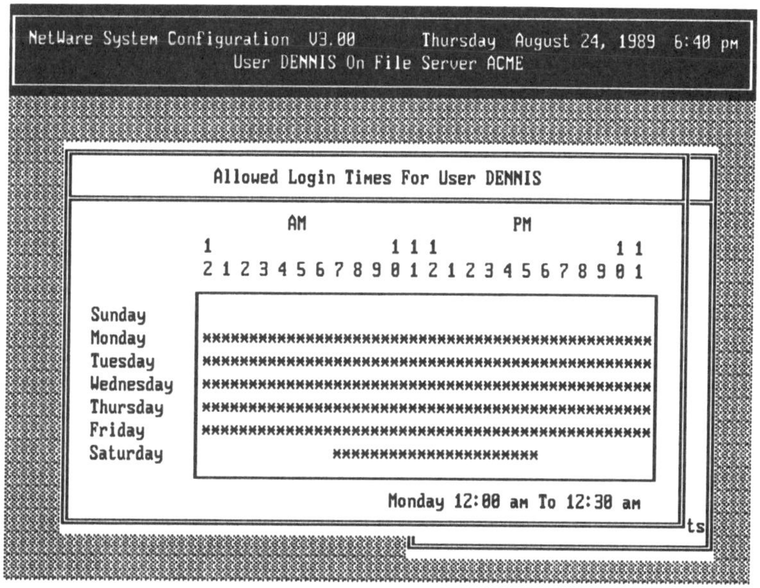

Figure 4.7 SYSCON Time Restriction display.

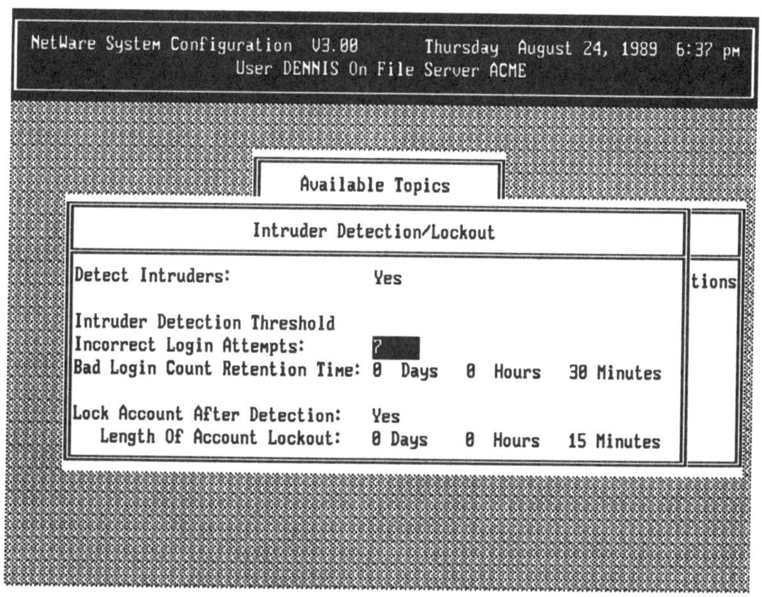

Figure 4.8 SYSCON Intruder Detection display.

Account Restrictions

Account Disabled: Yes to temporarily remove access to an account, No to reinstate a disabled account

Account has Expiration date: Yes to make an account temporary; set the expiration date (default is first day, next month); No to remove an expiration date.

Limit Concurrent Connections: Yes to limit the number of locations a user can log in from, set the number (1 to 100); No to leave the limit at 100.

Require Password: Yes to require a password; No to give the user the choice of having a password or login with just his or her user name.

Minimum Password Length (if password required): Defaults to five characters; type a new value.

Force Periodic Password Changes (if password required): Yes sets the default to 40 days after initial login user name was created and periodically 40 days thereafter and is recommended for better security. Number of days can be changed. No does not require the user to change the password.

Limit Grace Logins (if password required): Allows the user a fixed number of grace logins before he or she must change the password after it has expired.

Require Unique Passwords (if password required): No is the default to not request unique passwords after each password expires. Yes tests each new password against the last 10 passwords for duplicates and disallows usage if found.

Disk Resource Limitation: Yes specifies a limit to set space on the file server in KB rounded up to the nearest 4KB when you save changes. No allows the user to store files in his or her directories without a size limit.

To set default account balances:

TYPE/PRESS	RESULT:
SYSCON [Enter]	Displays the SYSCON menu
S [Enter]	Selects Supervisor Options
D [Enter]	Selects Default Account Restrictions
change the settings	Sets the account restrictions
Esc	Displays Change All Marker Users Restrictions to These settings box
Y [Enter]	Saves the changes

To set account restrictions for one or more users using SYSCON

TYPE/PRESS	RESULT:
SYSCON [Enter]	Displays the SYSCON menu
U [Enter]	Selects User Information
mark each user name F5 [Enter]	Selects user name to set restrictions
A [Enter]	Selects Account Restrictions
change the settings	Sets the account restrictions
Esc	Saves the changes

Time Restrictions

To set default time balances

TYPE/PRESS	RESULT:
SYSCON [Enter]	Displays the SYSCON menu
S [Enter]	Selects Supervisor Options
T [Enter]	Selects Time Restrictions
mark the block of time you do NOT want users to have access to using F5 Mark key and press DEL	Sets the time restrictions
Esc	Saves the changes

To set time restrictions for one or more users using SYSCON

TYPE/PRESS	RESULT:
SYSCON [Enter]	Displays the SYSCON menu
U [Enter]	Selects User Information
mark each user name F5 [Enter]	Selects user name to set restrictions
A [Enter]	Selects Restrictions
mark the block of time you do NOT want users to have access to using F5 Mark key and press DEL	Sets the time restrictions
Esc	Saves the changes

Station Restrictions

To find out what station addresses are assigned to each logged in workstation on the network type from DOS

```
USERLIST/A [Enter]
```

To set a station restriction to one or more stations for one or more users using SYSCON

TYPE/PRESS	RESULT:
SYSCON [Enter]	Displays the SYSCON menu
U [Enter]	Selects User Information
mark each user name F5 [Enter]	Selects user name to set restrictions
S [Enter]	Selects Station Restrictions
INS	Displays a Network Address entry box
type hex network address [Enter]	Selects the network address to allow access to
N [Enter]	Confirms to allow certain nodes; displays a Node Address box
type hex node address [Enter]	Selects the node address to allow as a workstation
INS type a new allowable node address [Enter]	Selects another allowable node
Esc	Saves changes

To delete a station (allowed node)

TYPE/PRESS	RESULT:
SYSCON [Enter]	Displays the SYSCON menu
U [Enter]	Selects User Information
mark each user name F5 [Enter]	Selects user name to cancel restrictions
S [Enter]	Selects Station Restrictions
select hex node address [Enter]	Selects the node address to remove access to
DEL	Deletes the node address
Y [Enter]	Confirms the command
Esc	Saves changes

Setting Intruder Detection

You can set the following using intruder detection:

Detect Intruder: Yes is the default that records repeated login attempts and displays Threshold settings; No stops recording login attempts and ensures no user will be locked out.

Incorrect Login Attempts: Default is to allow seven attempts before assigning intruder status to the login user ID. Can be set to a new value.

Bad Login Count Retention: Default is to keep track of incorrect logins for 30 minutes. Can be set to days, hours, or minutes to increase security.

Lock Account after Detection: Yes is default to lock the account if any of the above three set intruder status on the login account. No tells NetWare to ignore the feature and not lock out users with intruder status on their accounts.

Length of Account Lockout: Default is set to lock the account for 15 minutes after user ID has intruder status. Can be set to days, hours, or minutes for increased security.

To set intruder detection for all accounts

TYPE/PRESS	RESULT:
SYSCON [Enter]	Displays the SYSCON menu
S [Enter]	Selects Supervisor Options
I [Enter]	Selects Intruder Detection/Lockout
change the settings	Sets the account restrictions
Esc	Updates the screen
Esc	Saves the changes

Unlocking Intruder Detection

Hint: To view which users are locked out and why, examine the error log using SYSCON. See "Error Handling."

To unlock a user who is locked out

TYPE/PRESS	RESULT:
SYSCON [Enter]	Displays the SYSCON menu
U [Enter]	Selects User Information
mark user	
name F5 [Enter]	Selects user name to unlock
I [Enter]	Selects Intruder Lockout Status
N [Enter]	Selects the No for Account Locked
Esc	Resets status

Viewing the Last Login for a User

To view a user's last login date and time

TYPE/PRESS	RESULT:
SYSCON [Enter]	Displays the SYSCON menu
U [Enter]	Selects User Information
mark user	
name F5 [Enter]	Selects user name to view
O [Enter]	Selects Other Information
Esc	Returns to the menu

Mapping Logical and Search Drives

Purpose: To temporarily or permanently assign a drive letter to a specific directory path located on a file server for easier access (logical map) or search for programs (search map). Before you can work in a network directory, you must have a drive mapped to that directory. Used when adding a new user, application or data directory to the network.

Logical drives are used to access any subdirectory path located on a file server in a shortcut manner. They are conceptual rather than physical because they utilize up to 22 drive letters (F through Z) even though the network does not contain 22 physical disk drives. If you use letters A through E (used typically to point to local drives) with MAP, a prompt asks if you want to map the local drive to a network directory. A valid drive letter (F through Z) is used to create a drive that points to a file server subdirectory path, rather than a real disk drive.

For example, a path called SYS:APPL/WORDPROC could be labeled W for simplicity's sake as follows:

```
MAP WSYSAPPL\WP
```

Once this map is assigned, the user need only type W:CR to access this path. Thus, this method saves users from having to memorize the entire file server directory structure.

Search drives are used to tell the network where to look for program files with .EXE or .COM extensions on the file server. Once the directory with the files is found, the network accesses the files and starts the program. It is similar to using the DOS PATH command. Since the PATH command cannot be used on a file server, this command performs the same task. Instead of using a drive letter, you specify a search directory using a special name *Sx*, where x is a number from 1 to 26. Up to 16 of the 26 drives can be assigned as search drives. When you assign the first search drive, NetWare uses the last available drive letter. For example, the drive Sl would be assigned Z. If that letter has been used for a logical map, NetWare would use the next drive, Y.

To assign the program directory SYS:APPL \ WP as a search drive, type

```
MAP S1:SYS:APPL\WP [Enter]
```

Once this map is assigned, you can execute the program located in APPL \ WP by simply typing the command, regardless of what drive or subdirectory is current.

Note: To see how NetWare searches for an .EXE or .COM file, use the SMODE command before executing the .EXE or .COM command.

Often when maps are assigned, you forget to look at the display or notice which drive letter is assigned to a subdirectory path. The next section shows how to identify your mapped resources.

Identifying Mapped Resources

To display a set of all current logical or search mapped drives after logging into the network, type

```
MAP [Enter]
```

This command displays the current drive mappings for all drives on the workstation. Undefined local drives (drives that have not been mapped to a directory) will not be displayed.

To display the resource assigned to only one mapped, logical or search drive after logging in, type

```
MAP drive: [Enter]
```

If a map does not appear or you want to assign one temporarily, you can do so from the DOS prompt. The next section lists all commands that are used to set a map online.

Setting a Logical or Search Directory for a Work Session

There are two ways to change maps for the current work session: the MAP line command and the SESSION menu utility. The easiest of these two is the SESSION utility.

Using SESSION

Purpose: Assigns or deletes logical drive or search mappings for the current work session using a menu utility, rather than line commands. Allows you to change the default drive or server for the current work session. Figure 4.9 shows the SESSION main menu.

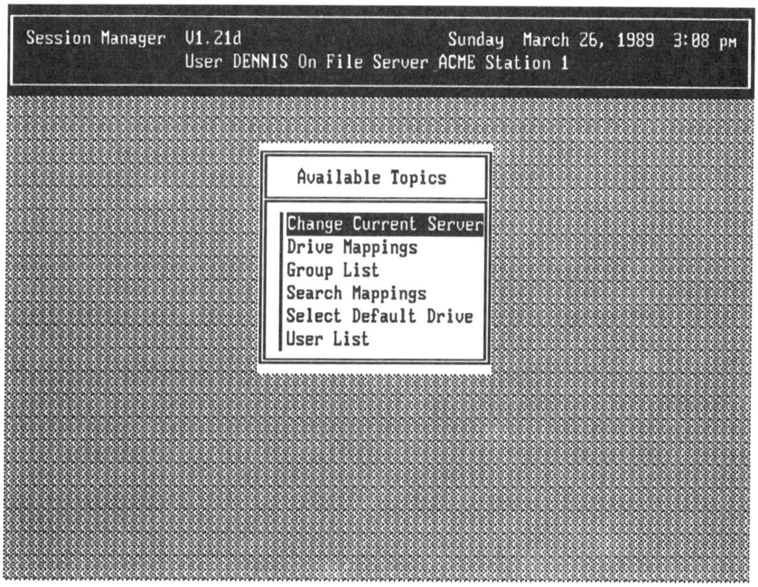

Figure 4.9 SESSION main menu.

To change a logical drive mapping with SESSION

TYPE/PRESS	RESULT:
SESSION [Enter]	Displays the SESSION menu
D [Enter]	Selects Drive Mappings command

To change a search drive mapping with SESSION:

TYPE/PRESS	RESULT:
SESSION [Enter]	Displays the SESSION menu
S [Enter]	Selects Search Mappings command

Using MAP

Purpose: Assigns one or more drives or directories to another from the DOS prompt. In each command, the *directory* parameter refers to the directory path, beginning with the volume name.

To assign the directory ACCTG located on the SYS volume, type

```
SYS:ACCTG [Enter]
```

To map a specific drive to a given directory, type

```
MAP drive:=directory [Enter]
```

To map the default drive (current drive) to a specific directory, type

```
MAP directory [Enter]
```

To map a specific drive to the directory that the default (current) drive is mapped to, type

```
MAP drive: [Enter]
```

To map one drive to the same directory as a second drive's map, type

```
MAP drive:=drive [Enter]
```

To map multiple drives to multiple directories with one command, type

```
MAP drive1:=directory1; drive2:=directory2;
drive3:=directory3 [Enter]
```

This command has the same result as executing the command `MAP drive:=directory` three separate times.

To insert a new search drive using the next available letter in the ordered sequence of search drives, type

```
MAP INSERT search drive:=directory [Enter]
```

To delete a MAP definition for a drive, type

```
MAP DEL drive: [Enter]
```

or

```
MAP REM drive: [Enter]
```

Frequently used maps are usually set by the systems administrator for each user and stored in an individual login script. These permanent maps or assignments are made when the user logs in and appear on screen quickly. Often you will want to verify a user's maps. The last section introduces the necessary commands to do this.

Setting a Logical or Search Directory in a Login Script

You can use the MAP command to permanently map a drive to a directory on the network. When you use the MAP command to save drive mappings in your login script, you don't have to remap drives to directories every time you log in. This command is useful if you frequently use a number of directories and don't want to specify drive mappings for them every time you log in. Examples of system and individual login map commands are shown in Chapter 2, "A Hands-on Tutorial."

To enter a map in a login script, you use SYSCON to call up the login script—either SYSTEM or USER (see the section on Editing Login Scripts). To type the map command, you specify the file server name in addition to the volume and subdirectory path syntax described in the previous section on entering a map command online.

Begin your first search drive map with S1; the first logical map can be any letter from F through Z. Often users can associate a letter with an application name. For example, W could map to word processing, S to spreadsheet, and so on.

To enter a search map command in a system login script, type

```
MAP S1 = FILE SERVER NAME/SYSPUBLIC/DOS__VERSION
```

This search map enables you as a user to access any of the DOS programs that are in the subdirectory DOS__VERSION, no matter what directory you were working in.

For example, a logical map command in a system login script could be:

```
MAP W:=FILE SERVER NAME/SYS:APPL\WP
```

This logical map command points to the directory name APPL\WP when the user types W:[Enter].

The next section shows a sample of maps saved in a system and individual login script.

Measuring Disk Space

Purpose: To keep track of the server hard disk space in order to prevent data loss, plan for expansion, monitor file size and applications program performance, and maintain organization of server hard disk.

Using VOLINFO

Purpose: Displays space allocation statistics for network volumes and directories.

To display statistics for the entire file server volume structure, log in as supervisor and type

```
VOLINFO [Enter]
```

Figure 4.10 shows a VOLINFO display.

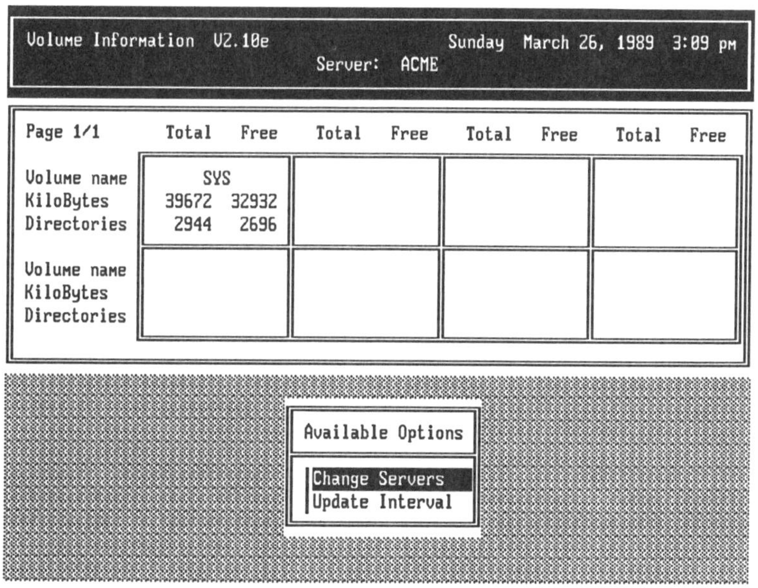

Figure 4.10 VOLINFO display for ACME.

Using CHKVOL

Purpose: Measures the amount of disk space available on a file server volume.

To measure the space used by volume SYS, type

```
CHKVOL SYS: [Enter]
```

A typical display of CHKVOL information looks like Figure 4.11.

```
Z:\PUBLIC\SHARE>CHKVOL

Statistics for fixed volume ACME/SYS:
  40624128 bytes total volume space,
   7159808 bytes in 279 files,
  33464320 bytes remaining on volume,
  33464320 bytes available to user DENNIS,
      2665 directory entries available.

Z:\PUBLIC\SHARE>
```

Figure 4.11 CHKVOL display for server ACME.

Using Keeptrack Plus

Purpose: To display or print a tree structure with utilization statistics for each file server disk directory. Also has file handling shell for copying, moving, deleting, renaming, sorting, searching for, backing up, or restoring files.

TYPE/PRESS	RESULT:
KT server directory [Enter]	Loads the program Keeptrack and examines the server directory
F2	Toggles on/off a detail directory display.
F3	Shows details for files such as byte size of each file, date and time it was last revised, and attributes of the file.

F4	Allows you to sort files by backup status, date/time, extension, filename, size in bytes, or physical location on disk.
Shift-F9	Prints All, Directory, Status, or Tree area to the printer.

A typical display of Keeptrack disk status and tree information looks like Figure 4.12.

```
GENERAL
    Total:  40,624,128  bytes        Verify: On
    Available:  32,641,024  bytes    Used: 7,983,104  bytes
    Total directories:  68           Total files:  263
UTILITIZATION
    Disk utilization:  19%           Files per directory:  3
    Files changed last week:  6  (2%)
    Files changed last month:  8  (3%)
```

Figure 4.12 Keeptrack disk status printout/display for server ACME.

For more information contact:
The Finot Group
2680 Bayshore Parkway, Suite 101
Mountain View, CA 94043
(415) 966-1900

Menu Designing

Purpose: To display a standard or custom menu for a NetWare-defined user group or individual upon logging into the system, or exiting one application. Interfaces between users and network to minimize learning time spent to start up and issue commands for the different applications and programs used on the network.

NetWare supplies a menu file called MAIN.MNU in the PUBLIC directory that executes each command menu utility programs. If you want to use this menu, don't name your menu file the same name. Although the NetWare-supplied menu is an excellent housekeeping tool, users are involved with many other tasks during a workday, such as using word processing, accounting, database, and other programs that cannot be accessed from this NetWare menu.

The NetWare MENU utility makes tasks such as the following possible:

1. Combining several NetWare utilities into one menu operation, speeding up access to and execution of command sequences that you use often.
2. Organizing certain infrequently used DOS and NetWare command line tasks within one menu. You can access the task from the menu rather than having to remember the command names, and you can use the menu prompts to issue command parameters (rather than having to remember the possible parameters or having to look them up in the manual).
3. Customized individual menus for beginning or occasional users who may not be very familiar with DOS or NetWare tasks.
4. Unique menu design so that every user can use a menu tailored to his or her specific needs.

NetWare Menu Syntax

To design a NetWare menu, you first determine the main or first menu's options, next decide which options of these are commands and which are submenus. You can skip ahead to Figures 2.15 to 2.19 to see an example of a main menu and submenus to practice design skills. To design a menu determine:

1. A menu title: The text and a line and row location to display the first line to include as the title for the menu.
   For example, the line:

   ```
   %EXAMPLE MAIN MENU,5,40
   ```

   ```
   "%EXAMPLE MAIN MENU"
   ```

   specifies the main menu title EXAMPLE MAIN MENU. The % symbol indicates that a menu name follows. Commas indicate that values follow. You can specify three values in this command line.
   The first two numeric values define the vertical and horizontal placement of the menu on the screen. A third optional numeric value defines the color palette. If you are using a monochrome monitor, you will not notice a difference if you specify a color palette. If you are using a color monitor, the color palette changes the color of the menus with the substitution of a different value from 0 to 7. You can add colors using the COLORPAL menu and pressing the INS key.

2. Each option on the menu. It can execute a program or command, display another submenu, or exit the menu. The order in which you enter options is not important; the options will be automatically alphabetized when the menu is displayed.

Menu titles and menu options must begin at the left margin. Do not use spaces at the beginning of lines, unless you are specifying a command. The % sign is a signal to the NetWare menu program that a menu title specification follows.

These next lines specify the menu options and tell the program that each is a submenu

```
System Accounting
 %System Accounting
System Applications
 %System Applications
System Remote Communications
 %Remote Communications
System Utilities
 %System Utilities
```

3. Each option to execute a program must include commands required to load the program. Commands include changing to the proper directory, calling the program, changing back to the root directory, and suppressing the screen display of commands.

Commands are identified in the text script file by indenting them two or three spaces. Include spaces only when they are necessary parts of the script.

These lines execute commands for the menu option WordProcessor

```
WordProcessor
  ECHO OFF
  CLS
  CD/WP
  wp
  cd/
```

The symbol @ places a message on screen with a command and waits to accept a response from the user. The user presses [Enter] to complete the response.

These lines show how to use @ to pause for various DOS commands

```
%System Utilities,5,70,
Copy Files
 NCOPY @1''Enter Source Dir/Filename'' @2''Enter Destination
Dir/Filename''
 DIR/W @1
 DIR/W @2
 PAUSE
DOS Execute
 @1''Enter Command''
 PAUSE
DOS Command Line
 ECHO OFF
 PROMPT TYPE EXIT TO RETURN TO MENU_DB
 COMMAND
 PROMPT MENU_DB
```

4. Each option to display a submenu should include a/sign in the title with a new vertical and horizontal coordinate and a color palette value. Its set of menu options follow the name. Each sub-option should include either executable commands or additional menus. It can also include a return option to allow the user to go back one menu level.

These lines show the placement of the four submenus and the options they display:

```
%System Applications,,5,10
WordProcessor
 commands....
DataBase
 commands....
Spreadsheet
 commands....
%Remote Communications,15,40
Carbon Copy
 commands....
The Coordinator
 commands....
%System Utilities,5,70,
Copy Files
 commands....
DOS Execute
 commands....
Format Diskette Data
 commands....
Format Diskette Boot
 commands....
Tape Backup & Restore
 commands....
```

Creating a Menu

Once you have determined the menu design, you create the menu using the steps that follow:

1. Type each line into a file with a text editor or word processor using an .MNU file extension in the name. You can use the MAKEUSER menu utility to create a text file. To do this, first type MAKEUSER [Enter], select Create New USR file, then type the text menu commands, press Esc to exit, and confirm the file save. Finally, rename the file using the DOS RENAME command to have an extension of .MNU instead of .USR, which is automatically added by MAKEUSER.
2. To display a menu after a user logs in, type the following in the last line of the login script:

```
#MENU ''MAIN''
```

MAIN.MNU is the file that stores the menu commands. The MENU utility runs the menus you create either from the DOS command prompt or a login script.

Hint: You need not run the menu from a login script. To run a menu from DOS, make sure the MENU.EXE file is located in the current directory or search path and type:

```
MENU menuname [Enter]
```

3. In order to use the MENU utility, these files must be in the SYS:PUBLIC directory:

```
SYS$MSG.DAT
SYS$ERR.DAT
IBM$RUN.OVL
SYS$HLP.DAT
MENUPARZ.HLP
MENU.EXE
MENUPARZ.EXE
```

4. Store the menu file that you create in the SYS:PUBLIC directory for everyone to have access to it. If you are making menus for each individual user on the network or just a few users on the network you can copy those menus into each user's HOME directory.

If you are familiar with DOS batch files, you can see similarities in how the Novell MENU utility works. Once you understand batch files, making and changing menus becomes very easy and you will find the management of the network easier also.

Figures 4.13 through 4.18 show a sample of the ACME main menu and four submenus designed with the Novell menu utility. To create this menu, you enter the lines shown in Figure 4.18 into an ASCII file using the NetWare MENU command utility or a text editor such as DOS EDLIN to create a file with an .MNU extension. You should locate the menu files in the PUBLIC directory or other common directory on the file server. Using this example as a starting point, you can experiment with different options to come up with a menu system that will work for you.

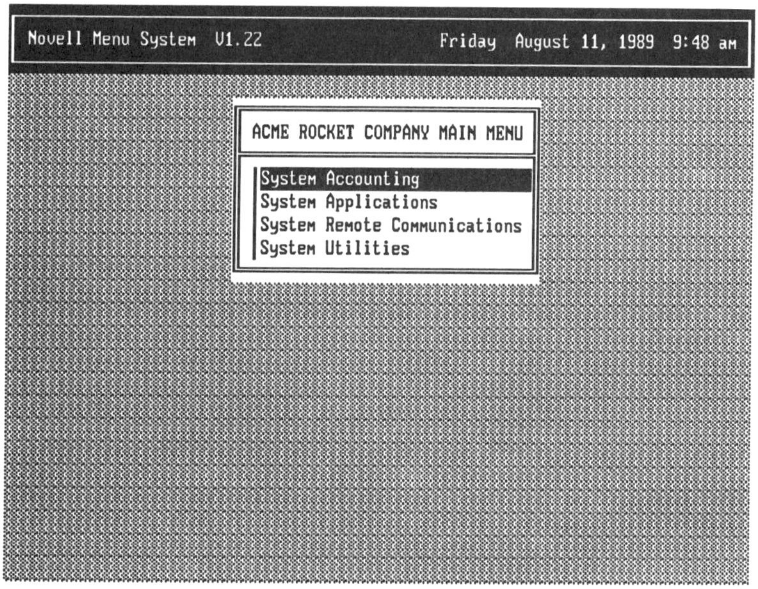

Figure 4.13 ACME Menu designed with Novell menu utility.

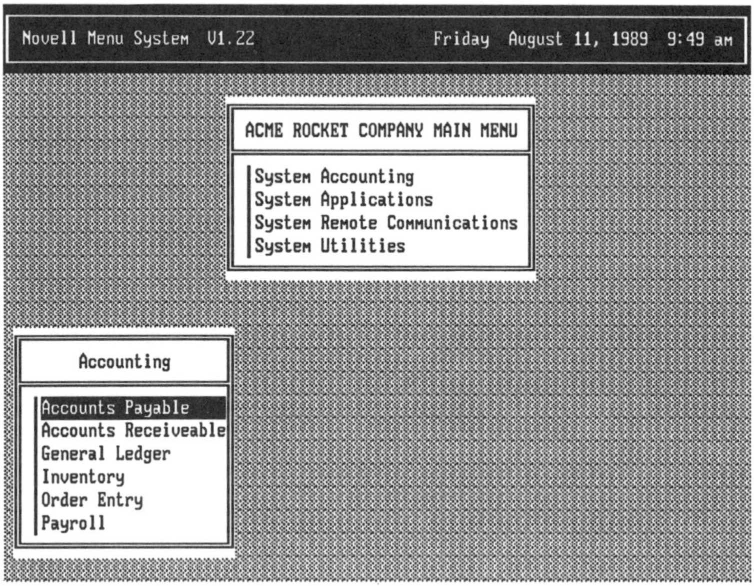

Figure 4.14 System Accounting.

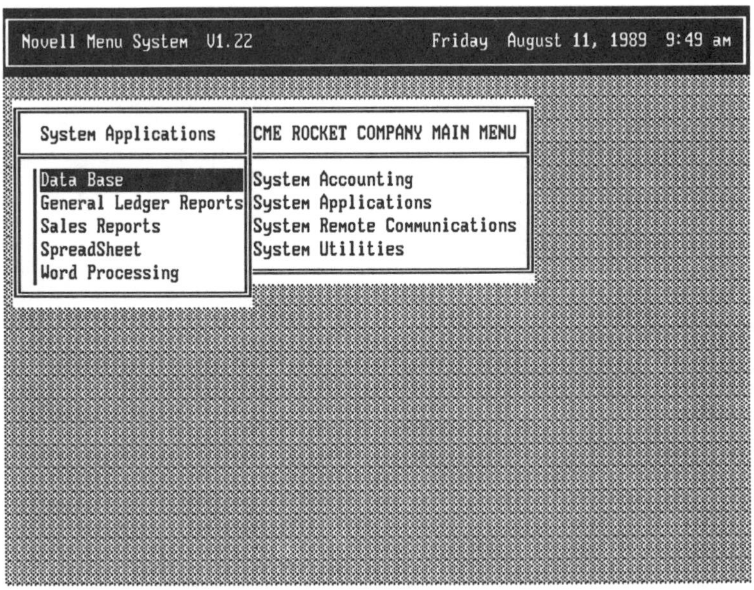

Figure 4.15 System Applications submenu.

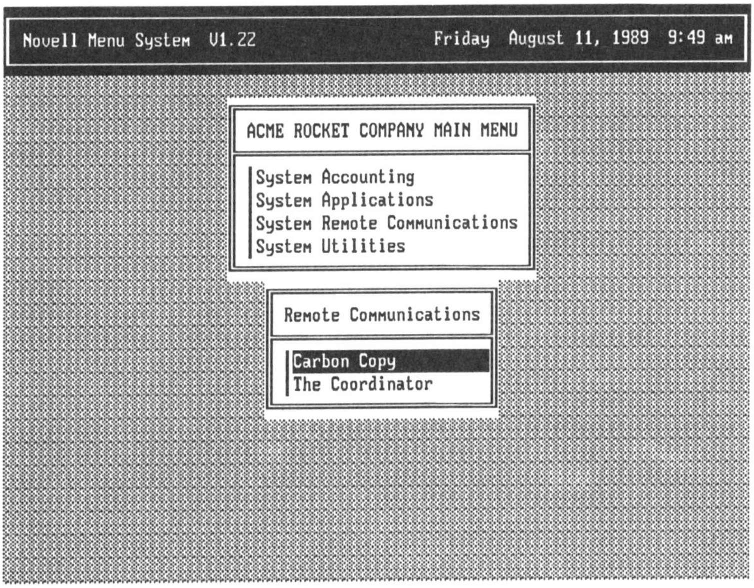

Figure 4.16 Remote Communications submenu.

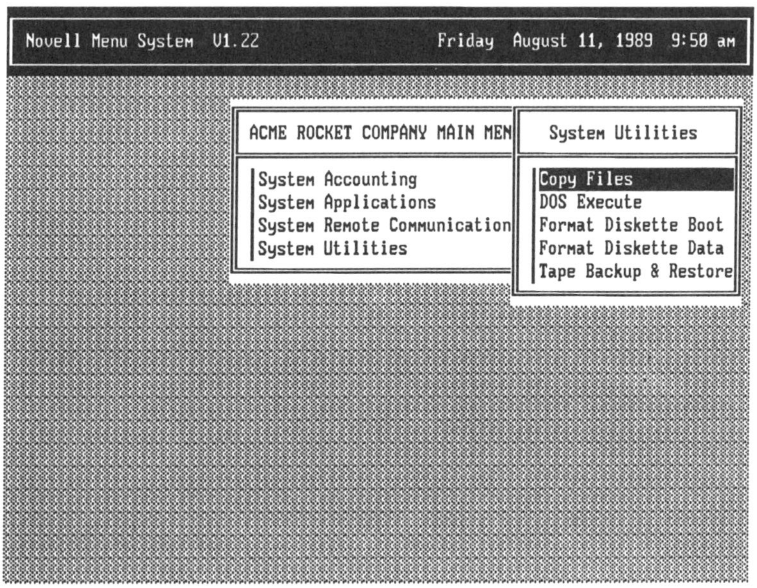

Figure 4.17 System Utilities submenu.

Listing 4.2 Menu example file ACME.MNU.

```
%ACME ROCKET COMPANY MAIN MENU,5,40
System Applications
 %System Applications
System Utilities
 %System Utilities
System Remote Communications
 %Remote Communications
System Accounting
 %Accounting
%System Applications,5,10
Sales Reports
 ECHO OFF
 CLS
 CD \ACCTG \SALES_DATA
 REPORTS
 CD \
General Ledger Reports
 ECHO OFF
 CLS
 CD \ACCTG \GL_DATA
 REPORTS
 CD \
Word Processing
 ECHO OFF
 CLS
 CD \APPL \WORDPROCESS
 wp
 cd \
Data Base
 ECHO OFF
 CLS
 CD \APPL \DATABASE
 DB
 CD \
SpreadSheet
 ECHO OFF
 CLS
 CD \APPL \SPREADSHEET
 SS
 CD \
```

```
%Accounting,25,10
Accounts Receivable
 ECHO OFF
 CD \ACCTG \AR_DATA
 AR
 CD \
Accounts Payable
 ECHO OFF
 CD \ACCTG \AP_DATA
 AP
 CD \
Order Entry
 ECHO OFF
 CD \ACCTG \ORD_ENTRY
 RUN OR
 CD \
General Ledger
 ECHO OFF
 CD \ACCTG \GL_DATA
 GL
 CD \
Payroll
 ECHO OFF
 CD \ACCTG \PAY_DATA
 PAY
 CD \
Inventory
 ECHO OFF
 CD \ACCTG \INV_DATA
 CAPTURE P3 NB NFF TI5
%Remote Communications,15,40
Carbon Copy
 ECHO OFF
 CD \CCOPY
 CC
 CD \
The Coordinator
 ECHO OFF
 ATC
 CLS
 CD \
%System Utilities,5,70,
```

```
Copy Files
 copy @1''Enter Source Dir\Filename'' @2''Enter Destination
Dir\Filename''
 dir\w @1
 dir\w @2
 pause
DOS Execute
 @1''Enter Command''
 PAUSE
Tape Backup & Restore
 ECHO OFF
 CD\TAPE
 TAPE
 CD\
Format Diskette Data
 ECHO OFF
 FORMAT A:
Format Diskette Boot
 ECHO OFF
 FORMAT A:\S
```

Note: Use SPOOL P=0 TI=5 command for CAPTURE in Version 2.0.

Once you have entered this text into a file, to display it as a menu, type

```
MENU filename [Enter]
```

You can also display a menu from a login script. (See "Login Scripts" for more information.)

Network Management using FCONSOLE

Purpose: To examine system statistics to maintain overall network performance.

Assigning a User or Group as FCONSOLE Operators

Purpose: To allow access to the file server console from any workstation on the network to issue commands to the file server and monitor network performance.

To assign a user or group as an FCONSOLE operator

TYPE/PRESS	RESULT:
SYSCON [Enter]	Displays SYSCON main menu
S [Enter]	Selects Supervisor Options
F [Enter]	Selects File Server Console Operators
Ins	Displays list of users and groups
select each user or group F5	Selects entities to allow as console operators
[Enter]	Completes the command

To remove the FCONSOLE operator status from a user or group

TYPE/PRESS	RESULT:
SYSCON [Enter]	Displays SYSCON main menu
S [Enter]	Selects Supervisor Options
F [Enter]	Selects File Server Console Operators
select each user or group F5	Selects entities to remove as console operators
DEL	
Y [Enter]	Completes the command

Using Statistics

To examine system statistics using FCONSOLE

TYPE/PRESS	RESULT:
FCONSOLE [Enter]	Displays FCONSOLE main menu
S [Enter]	Selects Statistics
S [Enter]	Selects Summary

A screen similar to Figure 4.18 appears.

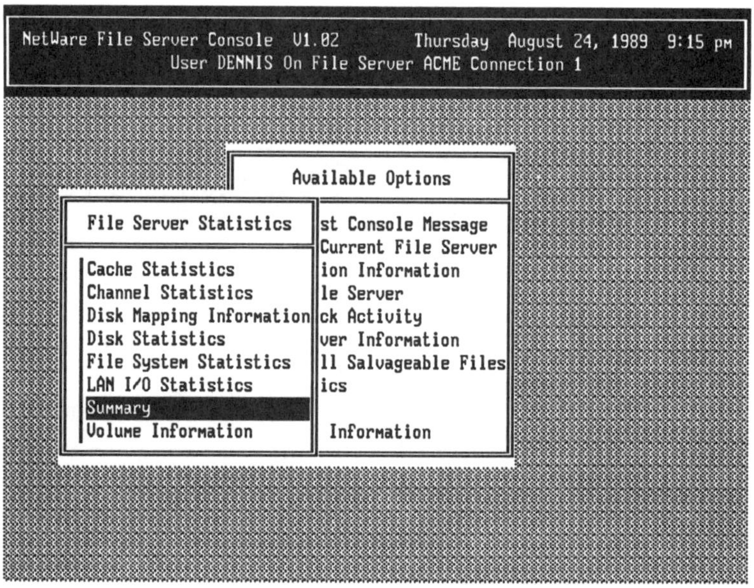

Figure 4.18A FCONSOLE (a) main menu and (b) summary of statistics.

```
NetWare File Server Console  V1.02        Thursday  August 24, 1989  9:15 pm
              User DENNIS On File Server ACME Connection 1

                     File Server Statistics Summary

File Server Up Time:    1 Day  12 Hours 13 Minutes  6 Seconds
Number Of File Service Processes:    10  Current Server Utilization:      7%
Disk Requests Serviced From Cache:  97%  Packets Routed:                   0
Total Packets Received:          33,490  File Service Packets:             5
Total Number Of Cache Buffers:       77  Dirty Cache Buffers:              0
Total Server Memory:          1,048,576  Unused Server Memory:         7,168

                          Maximum        Peak Used    Currently In Use
Routing Buffers:               40                2                0
Open Files:                   106               12               11
Indexed Files:                  0                0                0
Transactions:                 N/A              N/A              N/A
Bindery Objects:              N/A              N/A              N/A
Connections:                   32                1                1
Dynamic Memory 1:          19,408            3,060            1,440
Dynamic Memory 2:          11,644            2,270            2,208
Dynamic Memory 3:          10,240              712              120
```

Figure 4.18B

Printer Management

Purpose: To control the flow of *print jobs* or special files created to transfer output to a printer across a network using either printers attached to a file server or a print server. Special flags or settings are specified to control speed, print forms, copies, printer number, type size, orientation (available on most laser printers to control direction of printing—either portrait or landscape), banners (pages that identify the user who requested the report), and timing of printing. Flags set with command line utilities are separated by spaces. Flags set within PRINTCON are set in a form. Once a print job is sent, it can be canceled or deleted, rerouted to another printer, assigned a higher or lower priority, or suspended using PCONSOLE.

There are several ways to control sending output to a network printer using NetWare:

- The PCONSOLE menu utility.
- The PRINTCON menu utility.
- The NPRINT command line utility.
- The CAPTURE/ENDCAP command line utilities.

Each of these methods is discussed in the sections that follow in order of ease-of-use.

Third-party vendors offer other print job handling programs used to make printing on a network easier. LANSpool is an example of one of these programs used to create a special method of configuring printers on a network known as a print server. It is discussed later in this section.

The supervisor is responsible for making sure that all users can print through the various network printers. An important main concept behind using a network that the systems administrator must keep in mind is that no printed output is sent directly to a printer on a network. The printed output is always first sent to a temporary file created for printing and then released by the network to a printer. This file is referred to as a print job.

The print queue is a line where print jobs are sent to while they await printing. The first request that arrives is usually the first handled unless a request with a higher priority arrives after it. All requests in the queue "wait" in line to be printed. The PCONSOLE menu utility can be used by the supervisor or users to manage jobs in the queue. Job status can be viewed, moved forward or backward, canceled, held, or changed otherwise. The following sections discuss how to use PCONSOLE, the file server console, or QUEUE (Version 2.0 only) to perform these print queue tasks.

Configuring print queues is discussed in "Printer Configuration."

Print Queue Management Using PCONSOLE

Purpose: Views, deletes, and changes the status of print jobs in a queue of a network printer. Also used to add a print job to the queue, rearrange print jobs, hold print jobs, and view currently attached print servers. Version 2.0a users should see each section after the PCONSOLE sequence is described since PCONSOLE is not available to them.

Note: PCONSOLE is also used to create, rename, or delete print queues other than the default and assign users and console operators to a queue. See "Printer Configuration" for more on setting up additional print queues.

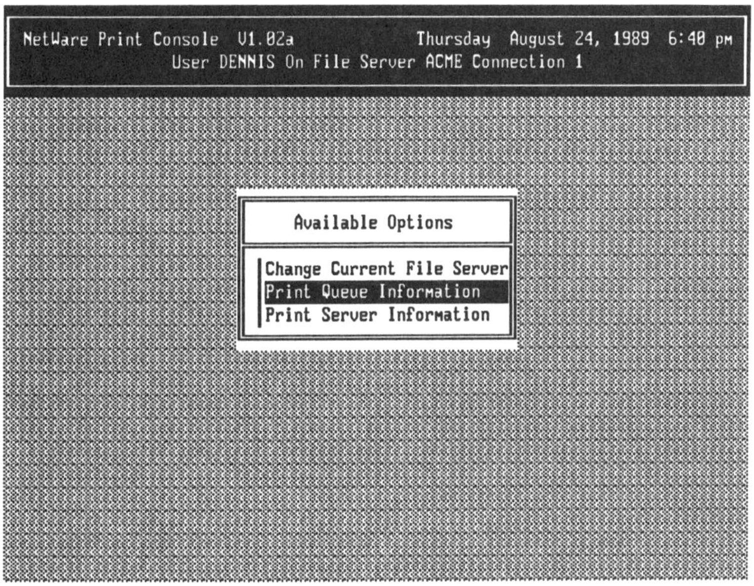

Figure 4.19 PCONSOLE main menu.

Listing Print Jobs

Purpose: Determines the status of a print job. Helps troubleshoot when a user cannot print to determine whether the problem is hardware- or software-related. If the print job is not in the queue, most likely the problem is software related. If the job is in the queue, it can be reassigned to another printer, held to examine the printer for hardware problems, or deleted. It is also useful in determining how many print jobs are ahead or behind your job.

To list all jobs using PCONSOLE in a particular print queue on the current file server

TYPE/PRESS	RESULT:
PCONSOLE [Enter]	Displays the PCONSOLE menu
P [Enter]	Selects the Print Queue Information option
select the print queue name to view [Enter]	Selects the print queue name to view
C [Enter]	Selects Current Print Job Entries option

Your screen displays a list of print jobs; it looks like Figure 4.20.

Changing Print Job Settings

Purpose: Allows certain parameters to be changed by the user who sent the print job to the queue or print queue operator. One good use of this command is to rearrange the sequence of print jobs. For example, if a large job is ahead of several small ones, it might be useful to hold the large job until the smaller ones are completed or move it to the end of the queue.

Description: Text description of file; default is filename.
User hold: "Yes" to place the printing on hold; "No" is the default and the way to remove a hold. Useful if a printer jams and you need to fix it.

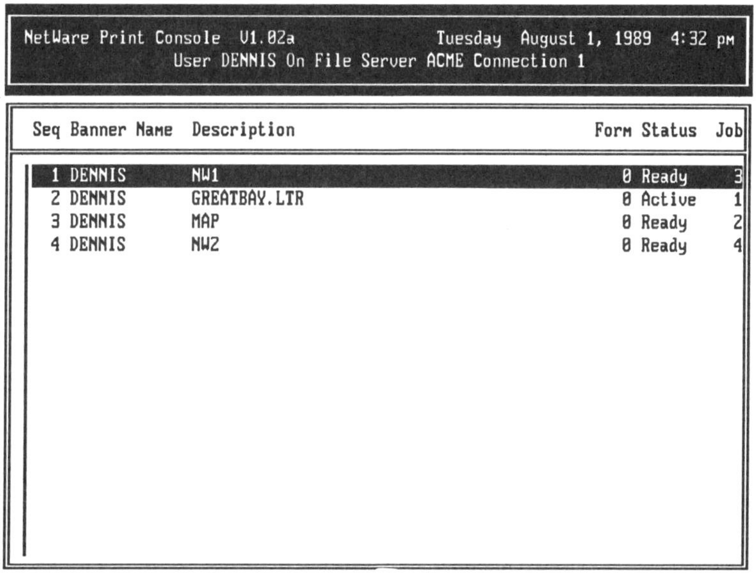

Figure 4.20 Print queue job listing.

Operator hold: "Yes" or "No" as with User hold but can only be changed by a queue operator.

Service sequence: Sets the position of a job to a higher or lower priority. Can only be changed by a queue operator. Typing "1" changes the job to the first position.

Number of copies: Sets the number of copies to print from 1 to 255.

File contents: Text or Byte Stream. Text is used for ASCII files; Byte Stream for applications. Byte Stream is the default.

Tab size: Used with the Text option of file contents to specify the number of spaces to expand the tab character in the file.

Suppress form feed: "No" to advance the printer to the top of the next page after the print job is completed; "Yes" to leave the printer after the last line printed.

Defer printing: "No" to print the job as soon as possible; "Yes" to print the job later.

Target server: Set to the print server that should print the job; if you have only one, the default is "Any Server." Useful if you want to send a job to another printer, rather than perform a time-consuming reprint such as with database or large-size data compilations.

Form: Sets the form number to print from 0 to 255; default is 0.

Print banner: "Yes" to print an informative banner with two large print areas; "No" to suppress banner printing.

Banner name: Sets a text banner name to print in the first large print area; default is user name.

Banner file: Sets a text filename to print in the second large print area; default is filename.

Target date: Sets a date to print the job; default is same as date sent.

Target time: Sets a time to print the job; default is same as time sent.

The PCONSOLE menu displays these settings as shown in Figure 4.21.

```
NetWare Print Console  V1.02a                  Tuesday  August 1, 1989  4:32 pm
                 User DENNIS On File Server ACME Connection 1

                        Print Queue Entry Information

Print job:            4                  File size:          13183
Client:               DENNIS[1]
Description:          NW2
Status:               Ready To Be Serviced, Waiting For Print Server

User Hold:            No                 Job Entry Date:     April 1, 1989
Operator Hold:        No                 Job Entry Time:     4:13:35 pm
Service Sequence:     4

Number of copies:     1                  Form:               UNKNOWN
File contents:        Text               Print banner:       Yes
Tab size:             8                  Banner name:        DENNIS
Suppress form feed:   No                 Banner file:        NW2

Defer printing:       No                 Target date:
                                         Target time:
Target server:        (Any Server)
```

Figure 4.21 PCONSOLE print job settings.

The following parameters cannot be changed:

- Job entry date and time.
- Print job number.

- File size.
- Client name.

To change the above print job settings using PCONSOLE for your own print job or for another user's job if you are a supervisor or print queue console operator (see "Printer Configuration" under PCONSOLE to specify a print queue operator) in a particular print queue, type

TYPE/PRESS	RESULT:
PCONSOLE [Enter]	Displays the PCONSOLE menu
P [Enter]	Selects the Print Queue Information option
select the print queue name to view [Enter]	Selects the print queue name to view
C [Enter]	Selects Current Print Job Entries option
select the print job entry to change[Enter]	Selects the print job to change
make the changes using the arrow keys or [Enter] key	Changes the settings
Esc once or twice	Completes the changes and displays a confirmation box
Y [Enter]	Confirms changes

Deleting a Print Job

Purpose: Allows you to cancel a print job due to duplicate requests, large size, or other reasons.

To delete or cancel your own print job using PCONSOLE or for another user's job if you are a print queue console operator (see "Printer Configuration (Network)" under PCONSOLE to specify a print queue operator) in a particular print queue, type

TYPE/PRESS	RESULT:
PCONSOLE [Enter]	Displays the PCONSOLE menu
P [Enter]	Selects the Print Queue Information option

select the print queue name to view [Enter]	Selects the print queue name to view
C [Enter]	Selects Current Print Job Entries option
select the print job with entry to cancel F5 DEL	Selects the print job to cancel
Y [Enter]	Confirms cancel

Using PRINTCON

Purpose: Used to control the way a job is printed in NetWare 2.1 and above. Sets flags similar to those set with CAPTURE as shown in Figure 4.22. Alters print job parameters such as banners, print queue name, and number of copies. Makes printing easier for less experienced users than using CAPTURE; the supervisor can create one or more print job configurations with all settings stored for each user. When the user prints a job using NPRINT or CAPTURE, NetWare looks at PRINTCON for a default print job configuration. It uses the default unless the user selects another. Once you have created print job configurations, they can be copied for each user.

The PRINTCON main menu looks like Figure 4.22.

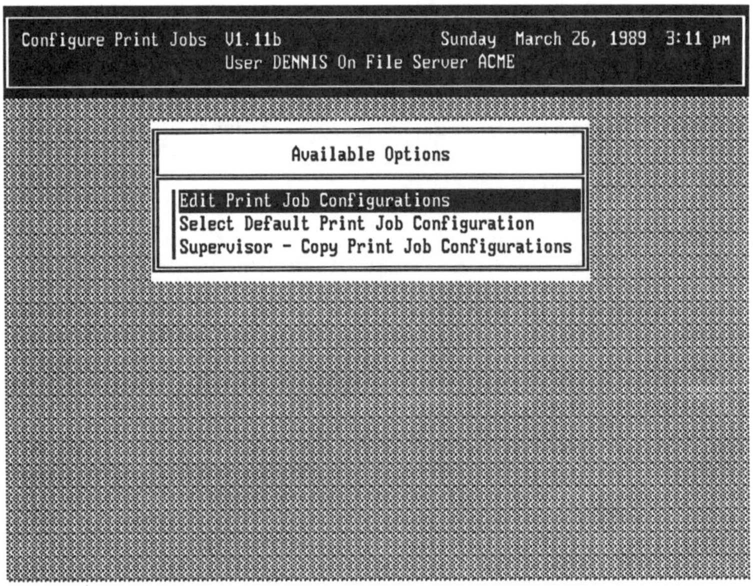

Figure 4.22 PRINTCON main menu.

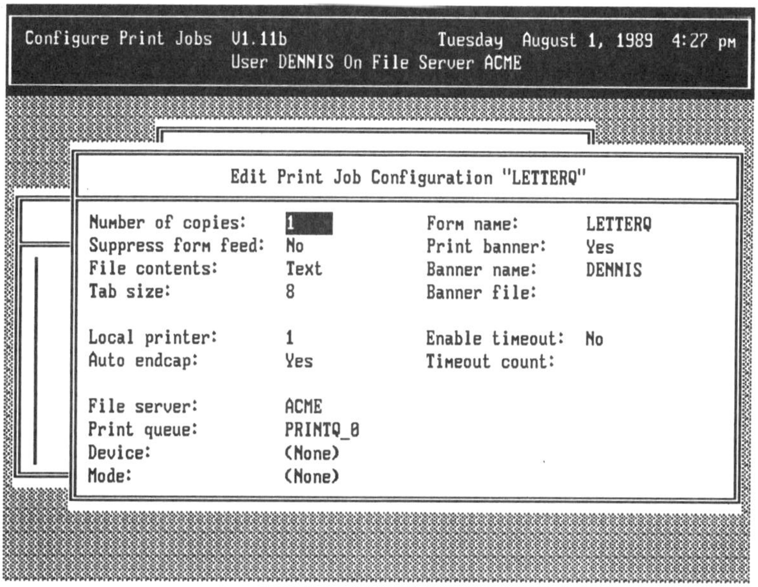

Figure 4.23 PRINTCON edit print job configuration screen.

Flags that can be set with PRINTCON are:

Number of Copies: Specifies the number of copies to print, 1 to 65,000.

Supress Form Feed: Sends a blank page after the file is printed to the printer. Type "Y" to suppress the blank page.

File Contents: Select Text or Byte Stream. Text is used for ASCII files, Byte Stream for files formatted within an application such as word processing, spreadsheet, or database programs. CAPTURE assumes Byte Stream; NPRINT assumes Text.

Tab Size: Sets tabs to a number from 0 to 18. If a tab character is included in the file, it is expanded the number of spaces needed to bring the print position to the next tab position automatically. Default is 8.

Local: Selects a local printer port LPT1 to LPT3 as 1 to 3; tells NetWare where to capture the file from (does NOT send the file to a local printer; see "Using the Network Assistant Plus" for details on sending a file to a local printer).

Auto Endcap: Affects jobs printed with CAPTURE only. "Yes" requests that the file you capture be printed after you exit the program. "No" specifies it to be printed only after you issue an ENDCAP command.

File server: Selects the file server where the needed printer is attached.

Print Queue: Selects a print queue name in place of a printer number (see "Printer Configuration" to establish a queue name).

Device: Press the [Enter] key to select from a list of printers that have been defined in PRINTDEF (if none were defined, you cannot change this field).

Mode: Press a letter key to select from a list of modes that have been defined in PRINTDEF (if none were defined, you can not change this field).

Form name: Selects the type of form from a list defined by PRINTDEF. Press [Enter] to view the list. Useful if you want the printer to wait until you change paper; the console will display a message to change the form and you must restart the printer after the form change. The printer will pause if another job arrives that requires a different form after printing of the file is completed.

Print Banner: "Y" specifies that a page with user ID name be printed before the file.

Banner Name: Specifies a different name for the upper half of the banner name up to 12 characters (replaces user name).

Banner File: Specifies a filename for the lower half of the banner name up to 12 characters (replaces the actual filename).

Enable Timeout: Select "Yes" or "No" (default) to have captured data print after the timeout seconds specified. Works only with print jobs created through the CAPTURE command.

Timeout Count: Used with a "Yes" value in Enable Timeout to enter a value in seconds from 1 to 1,000.

To set a default print job configuration for the network that NPRINT, PCONSOLE, and CAPTURE will use from the DOS prompt

TYPE/PRESS	**RESULT:**
PRINTCON [Enter]	Displays PRINTCON main menu

S [Enter]	Selects Select Default Print Job Configuration
select print job name [Enter]	Specifies a print job name as the default
Y [Enter]	Saves the changes
Esc	Displays Save Changes confirmation box
Esc	Returns to the PRINTCON main menu

To create a print job configuration using PRINTCON from DOS

TYPE/PRESS	RESULT:
PRINTCON [Enter]	Displays PRINTCON main menu
E [Enter]	Selects Edit Print Job Configurations
Ins	Prompts you to enter a new print job name
new print job name [Enter]	Specifies a new print job name
change the settings by moving the cursor to the item to change and press [Enter]	Changes the flags for the print job name
ESC	Displays a confirmation box to save changes
Y [Enter]	Saves the changes
ESC	Exits the PRINTCON menu

To edit an existing print job configuration using PRINTCON from DOS

TYPE/PRESS	RESULT:
PRINTCON [Enter]	Displays PRINTCON main menu
E [Enter]	Selects Edit Print Job Configurations
select print job name [Enter]	Specifies a print job name to edit
change the settings by moving the cursor to the item to change and press [Enter]	Changes the flags for the print job name

ESC	Displays a confirmation box to save changes
Y [Enter]	Saves the changes
ESC	Returns to the PRINTCON main menu

To delete a print job configuration using PRINTCON from DOS

TYPE/PRESS	RESULT:
PRINTCON [Enter]	Displays PRINTCON main menu
E [Enter]	Selects Edit Print Job Configurations
select print job name [Enter]	Specifies a print job name to delete
DEL	Displays Delete Current Print Job box
Y [Enter]	Confirms the deletion
ESC	Returns to the PRINTCON main menu

To rename a print job configuration using PRINTCON from DOS

TYPE/PRESS	RESULT:
PRINTCON [Enter]	Displays PRINTCON main menu
E [Enter]	Selects Edit Print Job Configurations
select print job name	Specifies a print job name to rename
F3	Executes the Modify command
Backspace	Deletes the old print job name
new name [Enter]	Renames the print job
ESC	Returns to the PRINTCON main menu

To copy one set of print job configurations from one user to another (note that the new file overwrites the old file of configurations) from DOS

TYPE/PRESS	RESULT:
PRINTCON [Enter]	Displays PRINTCON main menu
SU [Enter]	Selects Supervisor—Copy Print Job Configurations

type source user name	Specifies a source user name to copy FROM
[Enter]	Completes the command
type target user name	Specifies a target user name to copy TO
[Enter]	Completes the command
ESC	Exits the PRINTCON utility

Using CAPTURE

Purpose: Opens an output file to record data for printing. The file remains open until it is closed officially with the ENDCAP command. LOGIN, LOGOUT, and NPRINT NetWare commands as well as other utilities such as Network Assistant (see "Print Servers") also close the file because they automatically execute the ENDCAP command. This file is specifically created for printing and is automatically deleted after printing is completed. CAPTURE must be used when the application program you are using does not allow for a file to be printed to a network printer, or through the use of NPRINT. Version 2.0 users should note that CAPTURE is equivalent to SPOOL.

A typical program that cannot handle network printing is Lotus 1-2-3, Release 2. When you issue the / Print command, it does not allow you to specify the location of the printer. It assumes the printer is attached to the computer you are using, rather than a file server. Thus, the output will vanish if you do not invoke CAPTURE prior to issuing the /Print command, specifying that a file be created and which printer to send the output to. This is done before loading the application program from DOS.

A good way to ensure that a CAPTURE command is issued each time an application program is loaded that requires it is to design a menu for users that loads all applications. See "Menu Designing" for more on building menus. The command CAPTURE should be inserted before the command to load the program for each applications program that requires it.

Several flags or special settings can be set individually or combined using CAPTURE to control the way the file prints.

To combine flags using CAPTURE

```
CAPTURE /flag1 /flag2 /flagx [Enter]
```

To enter one flag using CAPTURE, use the reference below

Server: Selects the file server where the needed printer is attached.

```
CAPTURE S=server name [Enter]
```

Printer: Selects the network printer number 0 to 4

```
CAPTURE P=x [Enter]
```

Queue: Selects a print queue name in place of a printer number (see "Printer Configuration" to establish a queue name).

```
CAPTURE Q=queuename [Enter]
```

Local: Selects a local printer port LPT1 to LPT3 as 1 to 3; tells NetWare where to capture the file (does NOT send the file to a local printer but captures jobs sent to the local port and reroutes them to the specified network printer).

```
CAPTURE L=x [Enter]
```

Copies: Specifies the number of copies to print, from 1 to 65000.

```
CAPTURE C=x [Enter]
```

Job: Specifies a print job name (job names are defined using PRINTCON (see "Printer Configuration" to establish a print job name).

```
CAPTURE J=printjob [Enter]
```

Forms: Selects the type of form using a number 0 to 255, or form name; useful if you want the printer to wait until you change paper; the console will display a message to change the form and you must restart the printer after the form change. The printer will pause if another job arrives that requires a different form after printing of the file is completed.

```
CAPTURE F=form name or number [Enter]
```

Name: Specifies a different name for the upper half of the banner name (replaces LST).
Banner: Specifies that a page with user ID name and LST: be printed before the file. Can be used to change the LST: to a text name up to 12 characters or a user name other than the default.

```
CAPTURE B [Enter]
```

or

```
CAPTURE B=textname [Enter]
```

or

```
CAPTURE NAM=username [Enter]
```

No Banner: Cancels a banner page from being printed.

```
CAPTURE NB [Enter]
```

Tabs: Sets a tab to a number from 0 to 18. If a tab character is included in the file, it is expanded to bring the print position to the next tab position automatically.

```
CAPTURE T=x [Enter]
```

No Tabs: Cancels all tab expansions and interpretation of the character.

```
CAPTURE NT [Enter]
```

Form Feed: Sends a blank page after the file is printed to the printer.

```
CAPTURE FF [Enter]
```

No Form Feed: Does not send a blank page after the file is printed to the printer.

```
CAPTURE NFF [Enter]
```

Timeout: Issues an automatic ENDCAP and CAPTURE 1 to 1,000 seconds after the last character of a file has been printed to the CAPTURE file.

```
CAPTURE TI=x [Enter]
```

To view the printer(s) available for the current file server and their capture settings, type

```
CAPTURE SH [Enter]
```

This command should not be used separate from other CAPTURE flag commands.

Defaults for CAPTURE settings or flags are set to:

Server	Default server	Printer	0
Copies	1	Forms	0
Banner	LST:	Tabs	8
Timeout	0	Local(LPT)	1

To print a file using CAPTURE, type

```
CAPTURE flag1 flagx [Enter]
load applications program
issue print command
exit the application program to DOS (you can use a temporary exit)
ENDCAP [Enter]
```

To print a screen at a network printer using CAPTURE, type

```
CAPTURE [Enter]
Shift-PrtSc
ENDCAP [Enter]
```

(ENDCAP is optional if the timeout (TI) is set to a value other than 0)

Using ENDCAP

Purpose: Closes a file with data recorded for printing. If an ENDCAP is not issued after a CAPTURE, the file with the data to print will remain on the file server's hard disk until you either log out, log in a new user, or re-boot after turning off the workstation's power. Version 2.0 ENDSPOOL is equivalent to ENDCAP.

Several flags can be set using CAPTURE to control the way the file prints:

A	All: Closes the file and prints all data sent to print through LPT1, LPT2, or LPT3.
C	Cancel: Cancels the CAPTURE command and deletes all data sent to print to LPT1 (the default).
L=n	Local Selects LPTn as the source to capture data.
CL=n	Cancel Local Cancels LPTn as the source to capture from and deletes all data sent to LPTn.

Using NPRINT

Purpose: Prints an ASCII file(s) or text file(s) without special format commands. Most applications files you print are not formatted as ASCII; they contain special formats that only the applications program recognizes.

The easiest way to determine if a file is an ASCII file is to issue the DOS TYPE command. If it appears legible on screen, most likely it can be printed using NPRINT.

To view the contents of a file one screen at a time, type

```
TYPE filename | MORE [Enter]
```

The same flags or special settings can be set as with CAPTURE using NPRINT (except Timeout and Show) to control the way the file prints:

S	Server: Selects the file server where the needed printer is attached.
P	Printer: Selects the network printer from 0 to 4.
D	Delete: Specifies to delete the file after it is printed.
C	Copies: Specifies the number of copies to print from 1 to 65,000
F	Forms: Selects the type of form from 0 to 255 or name defined using PRINTDEF; useful if you want the printer to wait until you change paper; the console will display a message to change the form and you must restart the printer after the form change. The printer will pause if another job arrives that requires a different form after printing of the file is completed.
B	Banner: Specifies to print a page with user ID name before the file.
NB	No Banner: Cancels a banner page from being printed.
T	Tabs: Sets a tab to a number from 0 to 18. If a tab character is included in the file, it is expanded to bring the print position to the next tab position.
NT	No Tabs: Cancels all tab expansions and interpretation of the character.
NFF	No Form Feed: Sends a blank page after the file is printed to the printer.

Defaults for NPRINT settings or flags are set to:

Server	Default server	Printer	0
Copies	1	Forms	0
Banner	B	Tabs	NT
Form Feed	NFF		

To print a file to a network printer using NPRINT, type

```
NPRINT filename /flag1 /flagx [Enter]
```

Starting and Stopping Network Printers

Purpose: To start or stop a network printer due to a technical problem, testing, or to determine its status.

To start a network printer from the file server console

```
P x START [Enter]
```

where x is the printer number.

If there are no jobs queued, a message is displayed such as

```
"PRINTER x is running, no jobs queued"
```

To stop a network printer from the file server console

```
P x STOP [Enter]
```

If you stop a network printer using STOP, the jobs sent prior to the STOP will wait in the queue until the printer starts. New jobs will be sent to the stopped printer at the end of the queue.

Note: Version 2.0a users should see the Q command in the NetWare console manual.

Clearing Paper Jams

Purpose: Saves print jobs from having to be recreated if a network printer jams in the middle of printing.

To hold a print job using PCONSOLE

TYPE/PRESS	RESULT:
PCONSOLE [Enter]	Displays the PCONSOLE menu
P [Enter]	Selects the Print Queue Information option

select the print queue name to view [Enter]	Selects the print queue name to view
C [Enter]	Selects Current Print Job Entries option
Select first print job entry to change [Enter]	Selects the print job to change
change USER HOLD or OPERATOR HOLD to "Y" using the arrow keys or [Enter] key	Changes the settings
Esc once or twice	Completes the changes and displays a confirmation box
Y [Enter]	Confirms changes

To make a printer reprint a few pages of a jammed print job using the console command REWIND

TYPE/PRESS	RESULT:
P x REWIND n [Enter]	Rewinds printer x n pages

To reroute one printer to another temporarily to clear a paper jam that has lost several pages from the file server console using REROUTE, START, and STOP

TYPE/PRESS	RESULT:
REROUTE PRINTER x TO n	Reroutes print jobs from printer x to n
STOP PRINTER x	Stops printer and allows for clearing the jam
START PRINTER x	Restarts the printer on the network
REROUTE PRINTER n TO x	Redirects the printing of job back to the original printer
STOP PRINTER n	Stops the job from printing on printer n
START PRINTER n	Starts printer n

Printer Configuration

There are several ways to configure your network printers:

1. Attach printers to the file server only.
2. Attach one or more printers to a workstation and create a print server with one or more print queues attached; use print server(s) only.
3. Use printers on the file server and one or more print servers.
4. Attach to another file server and use its file server printers and/or print server(s).

Your system is using at least one of these options.

NetWare offers several tools to configure your network printers.

PRINTDEF: Defines each device model, its functions (escape sequences), and a set of modes and forms it can accept.

PCONSOLE: Defines print queues with print servers, user names, console operators, and output devices.

It does not offer the built-in capability to create a print server from a workstation. LAN Systems, a third-party vendor offers LANSpool, a utility program to create a print server or workstation with printers that can be used by any user on the network. Other vendors also offer this type of utility. Check with Novell for other products that perform this function or see "Creating a Print Server."

Using PRINTDEF

Purpose: Supervisor can define lists for users, and store *modes* of printing such as compressed, landscape, or final quality using control codes (escape sequences) and forms such as 8½" x 11" or 8½" x 14" for network output devices such as printers or plotters. Used by supervisor to define new device models not included in the PRINTDEF database of device models. New device definition requires entry of each escape sequence you want to define.

Figure 4.24 shows the PRINTDEF main menu, available only to Version 2.1 and above.

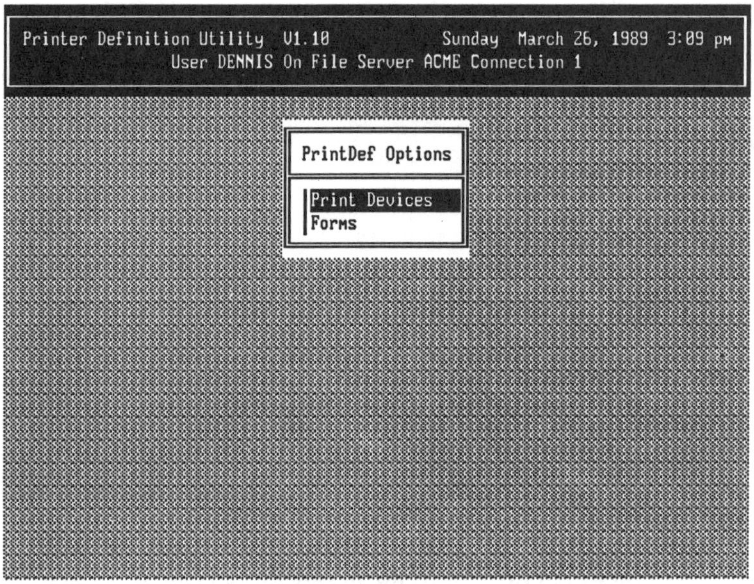

Figure 4.24 PRINTDEF main menu.

PRINTDEF includes a predefined database of devices and modes for many popular printer models. A device is the printer, plotter, or other output unit used by the network. A mode is a way of telling a device to print using an escape sequence made up of a series of control characters. PRINTDEF allows you to store these sequences as well as a description to identify the mode such as "Compressed" for an output device. Figure 4.25 shows a listing of modes stored in the NET$PRN.DAT file in the SYSTEM directory.

Your network consultant may have designed a custom device database for your system. It is a good idea to verify the devices and modes defined on your network. If your devices are not listed, you should define them using the PRINTDEF commands described later in this section.

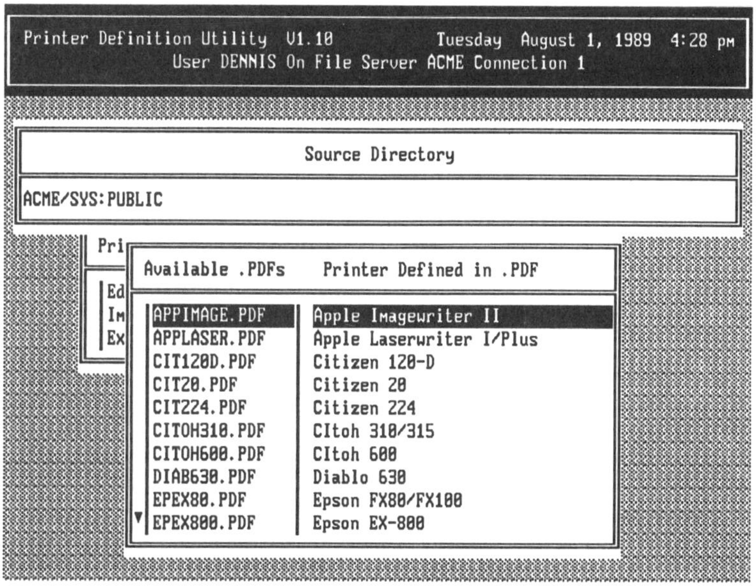

Figure 4.25 Database of PRINTDEF modes included with NetWare.

To verify if devices and their modes that are defined for your network, list each device and its modes using a user or supervisor login from DOS

TYPE/PRESS	RESULT:
PRINTDEF [Enter]	Displays PRINTDEF main menu
P [Enter]	Selects Print Devices option
select the print device to list modes for [Enter]	Selects a print device and displays Edit Device Options menu
D [Enter]	Selects Device Modes from the menu

A listing of modes should appear on screen for each device. You should make a print screen for each device and add this information to your systems documentation.

If you do not have a listing of devices, your system has not been configured using PRINTDEF.

Configuring PRINTDEF for the First Time

Purpose: To create a database of device names using functions to create device modes. The steps to configure network devices are:

1. Import the .PDF file for each device from the database NET$PRN.DAT file located in the SYS:PUBLIC directory.
2. Export to a .PDF file for each device from another file server's NET$PRN.DAT file. Import the .PDF file to the database NET$PRN.DAT file.
3. Create your own print device name, function, and mode table using the escape sequences from the printer manual.

The easiest of these is to import the .PDF file for each device from the NetWare database file NET$PRN.DAT.

To import the NetWare .PDF file from the original NET$PRN.DAT database file as supervisor

TYPE/PRESS	RESULT:
PRINTDEF [Enter]	Displays PRINTDEF menu
P [Enter]	Selects Print Devices option
I [Enter]	Selects Import Print Device option
SYS:PUBLIC [Enter]	Selects PUBLIC directory
type the .PDF filename [Enter]	Selects the definition to import

Note: See Figure 4.25 for a list of names. If your printer name does not appear, select a model that is similar to it. Consult your printer manual to find which printer operates in the same manner as your model.

TYPE/PRESS	RESULT:
[Enter]	Completes the command
Esc twice [Enter]	Displays Exit PrintDef confirmation box
Y [Enter]	Confirms exit
S [Enter]	Selects Save Data Base

If your printer does not resemble any of the listed printers enter the device name into the PRINTDEF database and the escape sequences for that device into its Function list.

To define a new device and its function listing for a new device as a supervisor, type

TYPE/PRESS	RESULT:
PRINTDEF [Enter]	Displays PRINTDEF main menu
P [Enter]	Selects Print Devices option
E [Enter]	Selects Edit Print Devices option
Ins	Displays a New Device Name entry box
type the new print device name [Enter] (less than 32 characters)	Enters a new print device name; displays Edit Device Options menu
select the new device name [Enter]	Selects new device name as device to define
Device F [Enter]	Selects Device Functions from the menu
Ins	Displays a Function Definition Form entry box
type a name [Enter]	Enters a name to identify the sequence
type the escape sequence [Enter]	Enters an escape sequence
Esc	Displays Save Changes confirmation box
Y [Enter]	Inserts and saves the new sequence and name into the Functions list
Esc twice [Enter]	Displays Exit Options menu
S [Enter]	Selects Save Data Base

Repeat this procedure for each sequence you plan to use including the reset sequence; check the printer or plotter documentation for a list of sequences.

Copying PRINTDEF Definitions to Other File Servers

Purpose: To copy one device definition from one file server to another. Use export to copy the device definition (one at a time) and import to add the device definition to the existing server's print definition database.

To export an existing definition from NET$PRN.DAT file to another server's .PDF file as supervisor

TYPE/PRESS	RESULT:
PRINTDEF [Enter]	Displays PRINTDEF menu
P [Enter]	Selects Print Devices option
E [Enter]	Selects Export Print Device option
select the device to copy from [Enter]	Selects the device to copy
[Enter]	Selects the current directory as destination

Note: To change the *destination directory*, press Backspace and Ins to display a listing of all directories. Press [Enter] to select the first directory and repeat the select and [Enter] process for each subdirectory.

Note: To change the *destination file server*, use the Backspace key and Ins twice to display a list of file servers. Select the file server by pressing [Enter] then type a supervisor login name and a password (if it's not attached to it). Select the directory using the [Enter] key and Esc, then [Enter].

type the export file name [Enter]	Exports the device definition
[Enter]	Completes the command
Esc	Returns to the Print Device menu

To import the exported .PDF file to the other server's NET$PRN.DAT file as supervisor

TYPE/PRESS	RESULT:
PRINTDEF [Enter]	Displays PRINTDEF menu
P [Enter]	Selects Print Devices option
I [Enter]	Selects Import Print Device option
select the source directory to copy definition from [Enter]	Selects destination directory

Note: To change the *source directory*, press Ins to display a listing of all directories. Press [Enter] to select the first directory and repeat the select and [Enter] process for each subdirectory.

Note: To change the *source file server*, use the Backspace key and Ins to display a list of file servers. Select the file server by pressing [Enter], type a supervisor login name and a password (if not attached to it). Select the directory using the [Enter] key and Esc, then [Enter].

type the .PDF file name [Enter]	Selects the definition to import

Note: You may need to rename the definition if an entry box appears. To rename it, type the new name and press [Enter].

[Enter]	Completes the command
Esc twice [Enter]	Displays Exit PrintDef confirmation box
Y [Enter]	Confirms exit
S [Enter]	Selects Save Data Base

Creating or Editing Device Modes

Purpose: Creates or changes existing device modes for a device such as compressed or other special fonts, styles, or orientations.

To define a new device mode for an* existing *device you create a mode name and select the proper escape sequences needed from the function list. You must be logged in as supervisor

TYPE/PRESS	RESULT:
PRINTDEF [Enter]	Displays PRINTDEF main menu
P [Enter]	Selects Print Devices option
select the print device to define new mode for [Enter]	Selects a print device and displays Edit Device Options menu
D [Enter]	Selects Device Modes from the menu
[Enter]	Confirms reinitialized mode in the Printer Device Name Mode box

Ins	Lists defined functions for the selected output device
select the reset function or escape sequence [Enter]	Defines reinitialization mode; displays the Printer Device Name Modes list

Note: If your printer does not use a single function for reset, you can mark each function needed with the F5 Mark key and press [Enter] to complete.

Ins	Displays a New Mode Name entry box
type the new mode name [Enter]	Enters the new mode name
Ins	Displays a list of all defined functions or codes for that device
F5 Mark each function	Selects each function for the r mode
[Enter]	Completes the command
Y [Enter]	Confirms save and displays PRINTDEF menu
Esc twice [Enter]	Displays Exit Options menu
S [Enter]	Selects Save Data Base

Figure 4.26 shows a listing of functions for an HP Laser Jet printer.

To list or edit the codes defined for each mode as either supervisor or user:

TYPE/PRESS	RESULT:
PRINTDEF [Enter]	Displays PRINTDEF main menu
P [Enter]	Selects Print Devices option
select the print device to list modes for [Enter]	Selects a print device and displays Edit Device Options menu
D [Enter]	Selects Device Modes from the menu

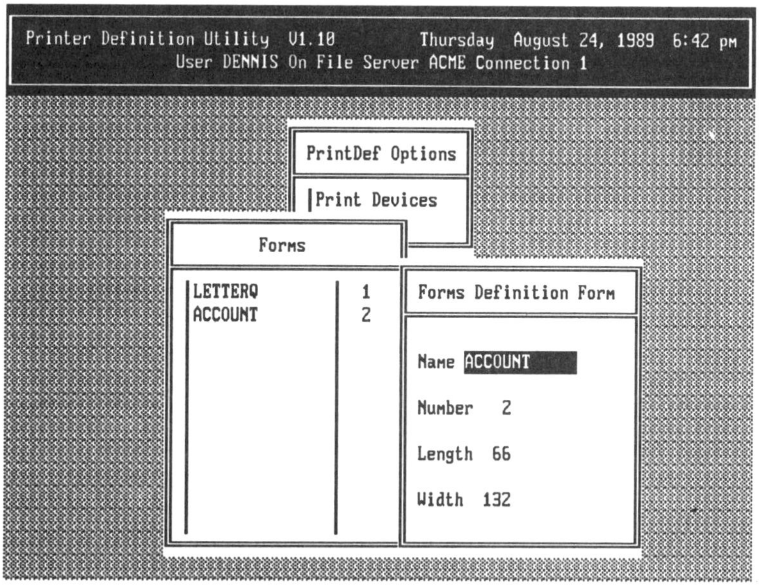

Figure 4.26 Functions defined in PRINTDEF for an HP printer.

The Device Mode Names and escape sequences are displayed. Note that you can view a long sequence in an inset box by moving the cursor to it and pressing [Enter].

These names or functions can also be edited using the arrow keys.

These also should be documented in your systems notebook by using the Print Screen key to print them.

Creating and Editing Forms with PRINTDEF

Purpose: To create a name for a special form type, such as continuous, labels, or other type or form name.

To define a form using PRINTDEF as a supervisor

TYPE/PRESS	**RESULT:**
PRINTDEF [Enter]	Displays PRINTDEF menu
F [Enter]	Selects Forms option

Ins	Displays a Forms Definition entry box
type the new form name less than 12 characters [Enter]	Enters the new form name
type the form number from 1 to 255	Enters the new form number
type the width in characters of the form [Enter]	Enters the new form width
Esc	Displays a confirmation box to save
Y [Enter]	Confirms save and displays PRINT-DEF menu
Esc twice [Enter]	Displays Exit Options menu
S [Enter]	Selects Save Data Base

Configuring Print Queues Using PCONSOLE

Purpose: Creates, renames, and deletes print queues. Assigns users who can place print jobs in each queue. Assigns users who can control each queue. If using PRINTCON to assign a job configuration to a queue other than the default, queues should be set up first with PCONSOLE. Queue configuration is available only to the supervisor.

To create a print queue using PCONSOLE

TYPE/PRESS	RESULT:
PCONSOLE [Enter]	Displays PCONSOLE main menu
P [Enter]	Selects Print Queue Information
Ins	Displays a New Print Queue Name entry box
type new name [Enter]	Enters new queue name

To make the new queue functional, attach the queue to a network printer at the console using the command

```
P x ADD queue name [Enter]
```

where x is the printer number and queue name is the new queue. To make this assignment automatically, edit the AUTOEXEC.SYS file found on the file server in the SYSTEM directory. To edit the AUTOEXEC.SYS file, use a text editor or SYSCON. If you do not assign queues for each printer, the system will create one for each network printer.

To assign queue users

TYPE/PRESS	RESULT:
PCONSOLE [Enter]	Displays PCONSOLE main menu
P [Enter]	Selects Print Queue Information
select the queue [Enter]	Selects a print queue to add users to
Queue U [Enter]	Selects Queue Users option

Note: When you create a queue, the user list defaults to the group EVERYONE. To restrict its use, use DEL to delete the group EVERYONE and Ins to access the user list.

Ins	Displays user list
select each user with the Mark key	Selects users for the queue
[Enter]	Completes the command
Esc	Returns to menu

Note: You can select a group as a queue user.

To assign queue operators to all queues (you cannot assign operators to one queue)

TYPE/PRESS	RESULT:
PCONSOLE [Enter]	Displays PCONSOLE main menu
P [Enter]	Selects Print Queue Information
Q [Enter]	Selects Queue Operators option
Ins	Displays queue operator list
select each user with the Mark key	Selects users for the Queue Operators Candidate list
[Enter]	Completes the command
Esc	Returns to menu

To rename a queue

TYPE/PRESS	RESULT:
PCONSOLE [Enter]	Displays PCONSOLE main menu
P [Enter]	Selects Print Queue Information
select the queue and press Modify (press Fl twice to find Modify key)	Selects a print queue to rename
type the new name [Enter]	Enters new queue name
Esc	Returns to menu

To delete a queue

TYPE/PRESS	RESULT:
PCONSOLE [Enter]	Displays PCONSOLE main menu
P [Enter]	Selects Print Queue Information
select the queue and press DEL	Selects a print queue to delete
Y [Enter]	Confirms deletion
Esc	Returns to menu

Creating a Print Server

Purpose: To allow the network to use an additional printer(s) attached to a workstation rather than a file server. Minimizes memory used by a workstation to access the print server. Maintains NetWare security by requiring a user login ID to attach the workstation to the network with limited rights that logs into the network to load the utility and then out. Resembles NetWare commands, making it easy to install and load.

There are several utilities that can be used to create a print server:

Product: Network Assistant Plus
Company: Cybertek LAN Software Inc.
Address: 6133 Bristol Pkwy.
Culver City, CA 90230
Telephone: (800) 533-4780
Price: $495

Product: PS-Print
Company: Brightwork Development Inc.
Address: P.O. Box 8728
Red Bank, NJ 07701
Telephone: (800) 552-9876
Price: $595

Product: ManyLink for NetWare
Company: NetLine Inc.
Address: 2155 N. 200 W., Suite 90
Provo, UT 84603
Telephone: (801) 373-6000
Price: $495

Product: Q Assist or Printer Assist
Company: Fresh Technology Group Inc.
Address: 1478 North Tech Blvd., Suite 101
Gilbert, AZ 85234
Telephone: (602) 497-4200
Price: $99 each

Product: LANSpool
Company: LAN Systems
Address: 599 Broadway
New York, NY 10012
Telephone: 800-827-LANS
Price: $395

Table 4.4 compares features from the above products.

The product LANSpool, voted product of the year in 1988 by *LAN Magazine*, is recommended for networks that need to keep memory used by the workstation to access the print server to a minimum. It works with Version NetWare 2.1 and above. Its installation procedure is very simple.

Table 4.4 Printer-Sharing Features

Feature	Explanation	Network Assistant	PS-Print	ManyLink	Printer Assist	LANSpool
Printers per workstation	The number of printers that can be attached to a workstation and shared.	1	5	3	15[1]	5.7[2]
Interrupt-driven parallel port required	Requires that workstation sharing a parallel printer use interrupt-driven parallel ports.	No	Yes	No	No	No
Pop-up printer console	A memory-resident module that runs at the workstation sharing a printer; allows users to view the status of the shared printer, start and stop it, and change forms	Yes	Yes	No	No[3]	No
Rewindable print jobs	A feature in the printer console that allows users to rewind the current print job to clear a printer jam.	No	Yes	No	No	No
Printer speed control	Allows users to control how fast a workstation drives a shared printer.	Yes	No	No	Yes	No
Forms control	Allows correct form type to be mounted.	Yes	Yes	No	No	No[4]
Queuing method	How the print queues are handled; some products use the same method found in NetWare 2.1. Products that use proprietary queuing methods are compatible with NetWare 2.0 and 2.1.	Proprietary	NetWare 2.1	Proprietary	Proprietary	NetWare 2.1
Queues per printer	The number of print queues a printer can service.	1	Up to 5	1	Up to 3[5]	Unlimited[4]
Queue priorities	Allows users to set queue priorities so some jobs print sooner than others.	No	Yes	No	Yes	No
User notification	The user is notified, via NetWare's SEND command, that a print job is done.	No	Yes	No	No	No
Non-dedicated mode	The workstation sharing a printer can still run applications while printing.	Yes	Yes	Yes	Yes	Yes
Dedicated mode	The workstation sharing a printer cannot run applications while printing.	No	Yes	No	No	Yes

Notes:

1. Additional hardware is needed to share more than five printers per workstation.
2. Five printers for non-dedicated servers: seven for dedicated servers.
3. Will be offered with the next version, scheduled for release in July.
4. The dedicated print server does recognize form control.
5. The new version, scheduled for release in July, will support five queues.
6. Limited only by NetWare.

To install the product LANSpool on your system

1. Copy LANSpool files to a file server volume and directory that the workstation is attached to.
2. Create a print server and a print queue name using PCONSOLE.
3. Create a new user with rights for the new print server workstation user ID login using SYSCON.
4 Log in at the print server workstation as the new user and load LANSpool.
5. Identify the printers attached to the workstation, define their communications parameters, and designate the print queues they will operate with.

Search Directories

Purpose: (See Mapping Logical and Search Directories.)

Security and Trustee Rights

Purpose: To assign rights to a directory for a user or group to protect the system against accidental erasing of files, creation of file directories, edits to files, and sharable status of files.

The eight directory rights a supervisor can assign using NetWare are:

R: Read From Files

W: Write To Files

O: Open Existing Files

C: Create New Files

D: Delete Files

P: Parental Rights

S: Search For Files

M: Modify File Names/Flags

To assign or remove these rights, you can use the SYSCON, MAKEUSER, or the GRANT, REMOVE, and REVOKE commands. Each of these is discussed further in the following sections.

Using SECURITY

Purpose: To flag items that could cause security problems: user names without passwords or names with passwords that are easy to guess: passwords that could have been changed in the last 60 days; users or groups with security equivalence to supervisor; users or groups with privileges in the root directory of the volume; users without a login script; or users with excessive rights in the PUBLIC, LOGIN, or MAIL directories. Displays the information to the screen only and works with all versions. Figure 4.27 shows a sample security screen.

To display security information from the SYS:SYSTEM directory, type

TYPE/PRESS	RESULT:
security [Enter]	Displays information on screen

```
        Does not require a password
        Has no password assigned
User DENNIS
        Has no login script
        Is security equivalent to user SUPERVISOR
        Has unlimited grace logins
        Is not required to change passwords periodically
        Can have passwords that are too short (less than 5)
User GUEST
        Has no login script
        Has no password assigned
User SUPERVISOR
        Has no login script
        Has unlimited grace logins
        Is not required to change passwords periodically
        Can have passwords that are too short (less than 5)
        Does not require a password
        Has no password assigned

F: \ PUBLIC \ SHARE >
```

Figure 4.27 Sample SECURITY screen.

Setting Security Equivalences using SYSCON

Purpose: To set a user's security equivalence to that of supervisor, other user, or group with a higher equivalence.

To change the security equivalence for a user

TYPE/PRESS	RESULT:
SYSCON [Enter]	Displays SYSCON main menu
U [Enter]	Selects User Information
select user name [Enter]	Selects user to assign equivalence
S [Enter]	Selects Security Equivalences

Ins	Displays other users and groups
F5 to mark each user or group [Enter]	Displays user or group's security rights for equivalence level

Assigning or Removing Rights using SYSCON

Purpose: Assigns or removes individual, group, or system-wide rights for files and/or directories permanently.

To add the default directory rights for a user

TYPE/PRESS	RESULT:
SYSCON [Enter]	Displays SYSCON main menu
U [Enter]	Selects User Information
select user name [Enter]	Selects user to assign rights to
TR [Enter]	Selects Trustee Assignments
Ins	Displays box asking for directory to add the trustee
Ins	Begins building directory path by displaying file server name and /
type directory name or continue to press Ins, hihglighting proper directories and pressing until the full directory path name is created	Selects directory name to assign rights

The user will receive the default directory rights; all eight rights for Version 2.1 or Read, Open, and Search for Version 2.15.

To add another right for a directory

TYPE/PRESS	RESULT:
SYSCON [Enter]	Displays SYSCON main menu
U [Enter]	Selects User Information
select user name [Enter]	Selects user to assign rights for
T [Enter]	Selects Trustee Assignments

select the directory name [Enter]	Selects the directory and displays current trustee rights granted
Ins	Displays available rights to assign
F5 to mark each new right [Enter]	Adds marked rights to Trusted Rights Granted box
Esc	Updates granted rights in Trustee Directory Assignment box

To delete a right for a directory

TYPE/PRESS	RESULT:
SYSCON [Enter]	Displays SYSCON main menu
U [Enter]	Selects User Information
select user name [Enter]	Selects user to assign rights for
T [Enter]	Selects Trustee Assignments
select the directory name [Enter]	Selects the directory
F5 to mark each right to delete	Selects rights to delete
DEL	Displays Revoke All Marked Trustee Rights box
Y [Enter]	Deletes marked rights
Esc	Updates Trustee Directory Assignments box

Using MAKEUSER

TYPE/PRESS	RESULT:
MAKEUSER [Enter]	Displays MAKEUSER main menu
C [Enter]	Selects Create New USR file option
enter the following keyword:	

#CREATE username;full name;password;groupl[,groupN];+
trustee directory namel[rights][,trustee directory name2 + [rights]]

Creates a new user with info included between ; (semicolon).
To eliminate any option, leave a blank between each ;.

Esc	Completes entry of keywords
Y [Enter]	Confirms completion of entry
filename [Enter]	Specifies filename as .USR file

To process the .USR file from DOS

```
MAKEUSER filename.USR [Enter]
```

NetWare will process the commands and create the new user based on the information you have entered. This method is useful when adding multiple new users. See "Adding a New User ID" for other related keywords used with MAKEUSER's #CREATE keyword.

Using GRANT

Purpose: Assigns rights to trustees.

To assign rights for a user using GRANT type

```
GRANT all or no RIGHTS EXCEPT rwoscdpm FOR directory or drive TO
user or group [Enter]
```

See previous section "Using SYSCON" for a definition of RWOSCDPM rights.

Using REMOVE

Purpose: Removes a user or group from a directory path or trustee. You can use MAP to assign the directory path a drive letter.

To remove a user or group from a directory, type

```
REMOVE user or group FROM directory path [Enter]
```

Using REVOKE

Purpose: Done at the DOS prompt rather than in SYSCON. Deletes trustee rights of users or groups of users in a particular directory. Rights can be revoked individually or globally. Useful when a user or group needs exclusive access to a file or files in a directory. Saves time by revoking one or more rights from a directory with one command, rather than revoking it from each user's trustee rights, one by one. If a user needs a right that has been revoked using a global REVOKE command, use the GRANT command to re-establish the right. You can use MAP to assign a drive letter to the directory path.

To revoke a trustee right from a directory, type

```
REVOKE rwocdpsm FOR directory or drive FROM user or group [Enter]
```

Using RIGHTS

Purpose: Displays effective security rights for a user in a specific directory. You can use MAP to assign the directory path a drive letter.

To display your rights using the command RIGHTS for the current directory, type

```
RIGHTS [Enter]
```

To specify a different directory, type

```
RIGHTS directory or drive [Enter]
```

A RIGHTS listing looks like Figure 4.28.

```
Z:\PUBLIC\SHARE>RIGHTS
ACME/SYS:PUBLIC/SHARE
Your Effective Rights are [RWOCDPSM]:
  You may Read from Files.                        (R)
  You may Write to Files                          (W)
  You may Open existing Files                     (O)
  You may Create new Files.                       (C)
  You may Make new Subdirectories.                (C)
  You may Delete existing Files.                  (D)
  You may Erase existing Subdirectories.          (D)
  You may Change Users' Directory Rights.         (P)
  You may Search the Directory.                   (S)
  You may Modify File Status Flags.               (M)

  You have ALL RIGHTS to this directory area.

Z:\PUBLIC\SHARE>
```

Figure 4.28 RIGHTS listing.

Using TLIST

Purpose: Lists trustees of a directory and rights granted. You can use MAP to assign the directory path a drive letter.

To display trustees and rights using the command TLIST for the current directory, type

```
TLIST [Enter]
```

To specify a different directory, type

```
TLIST directory or drive [Enter]
```

A TLIST listing looks like Figure 4.29.

```
        J:\APPL\WORDPROC>TLIST
        SYS:APPL/WORDPROC
        User trustees:
         USER8_WP      [RWOCD S ]
         USER9_WP      [RWOCD S ]

Group trustees:
         EVERYONE      [RWOCDPS ]

J:\APPL\WORDPROC>
```

Figure 4.29 TLIST listing.

Note: When you grant rights to a user in a directory, the user automatically gains rights to all *subdirectories* under that directory. However, if you examine one of those subdirectories using TLIST, no trustees are listed. Therefore, users can accidentally gain rights to a directory simply due to someone else having granted rights in a parent directory. To avoid this, carefully plan your directory structure.

Hint: To revoke rights in a subdirectory for a user who has rights only because of a GRANT to its parent directory, regrant them using GRANT in that subdirectory (if you try to revoke them, you will oddly get a message that says the user is NOT a trustee), check with

TLIST to verify the assignment, and then use REVOKE to delete them. You could use TLIST once again to verify the REVOKE command.

Sending Messages

Purpose: To send a brief message of up to 40 characters to one or more users or a defined group of users. Can be performed by a supervisor or a user. At least one user of recipients must be logged in to receive message.

Using SESSION

To send a user(s) a brief message using SESSION

TYPE/PRESS	RESULT:
Session [Enter]	
U [Enter]	Selects User List
or	
G [Enter]	Selects Group List
select the user or group name using the ↓ or ↑ and F5 Mark key (press Help twice to verify this key as the Mark key)	Selects the user or group name
[Enter]	
S [Enter]	Selects Send Message
type the message (up to 40 characters less the length of your user name)	Specifies message to send
[Enter]	Completes the command

Note: If the user you are sending the message to has issued the CASTOFF command or if the destination of the message is a group without members logged in, the message will not be sent. A message appropriate to either of the two situations will appear on your screen.

Hint: To cancel the CASTOFF command, issue the CASTON command.

Using FCONSOLE

Purpose: To broadcast a message up of to 55 characters to all stations logged in. Uses the menu utility FCONSOLE.

To broadcast a message using FCONSOLE

TYPE/PRESS	RESULT:
FCONSOLE [Enter]	Displays FCONSOLE main menu
B [Enter]	Selects Broadcast Console Message
type the message [Enter]	Sends the message

Using SEND

To send a message with the line command SEND, type

```
SEND ''message'' TO user name or group [Enter]
```

Note that the message must be enclosed in quotes.

See "Electronic Mail" for more on sending longer memos and files to other network users.

SESSION Menu Utility

(See Mapping or Sending Messages.)

Shells (Network)

Purpose: To act as a translator between the NetWare software and DOS. The shell is a small group of files that resides at each workstation and uses about 40K of RAM memory. These files are:

IPX.COM

NETx.COM

SHELL.CFG

It interprets each command request made by the user and decides to direct it to either the file server or DOS. For more on generating a set of shell files, see Appendix B: Shell Configuration File Options, *NetWare Supervisor Reference*.

To load the shell create a boot diskette by copying the files SHELL.CFG, IPX.COM, and NETx.COM to either the floppy diskette or hard disk root directory. Then load the IPX and NETx programs.

Using IPX

Purpose: Loads the shell file used for internetwork package exchange (IPX.COM).

To load the first shell file IPX.COM for your workstation, type

```
IPX [Enter]
```

Make sure the file IPX.COM is located in the directory on the current drive.

Using NETx

Purpose: Loads the NetWare shell for DOS Version x at a workstation. Version 2.0x uses ANETx.

To load the second shell file NETx.COM for your workstation, type

```
NETx [Enter]
```

Your workstation should now be attached to the file server.

Hint: Create a NET.BAT file with DOS EDLIN or the COPY CON command with the commands:

IPX

NETx

Locate the NET command in your AUTOEXEC.BAT file.

Turning Off the File Server

Purpose: To issue a command to power down the file server securely and then turn off the electrical power.

To power down the file server, make sure all users are logged out using

```
USERLIST [Enter]
```

Use the SEND command to send the user(s) that are logged in a message to log out.

Once you are sure all users are logged out, use the FCONSOLE menu to power down the file server software

TYPE/PRESS	RESULT:
FCONSOLE [Enter]	Displays FCONSOLE main menu
D [Enter]	Selects Down File server

Trustee Rights

(See "Security and Trustee Rights.")

Workstation Lockout

(See "Station Login Restrictions.")

Error Handling

Purpose: To view any errors recorded by the file server in the systems log. Shows whether any errors occurred when the file server was booted.

Viewing the Error Log

To view the system error log

TYPE/PRESS	RESULT:
SYSCON [Enter]	
S [Enter]	Supervisor Options
V [Enter]	View File Server Error Log
Esc	Prompts you to clear the error log
Y [Enter]	Erases error log
or	
N [Enter]	Keeps the error log

Summary

This chapter has presented several tasks that the systems administrator will perform on the network. It has presented different commands to perform each task when possible. Rather than trying to identify every NetWare command, you now have a handy task reference in place of the set of manuals that NetWare provides. The next chapter deals with an intermediate to advanced task of adding a new workstation on the network.

Part III

Workstation Issues

Chapter 5

Adding a New Workstation to a Network

After taking an inventory such as the one outlined in Part I, you should recognize each of the hardware resources in your system. Managers often expect you to purchase, install, and reconfigure network workstations. As a systems administrator, you learn to handle the problems that occur on network hardware components by using the systems consultant, vendor technical support, and trial and error. After a short time, you develop an understanding of most of its components.

This chapter deals with adding a new workstation to your network. The following steps are discussed:

- Ensuring proper cabling.
- Identifying cable layout and network interface card type.
- Configuring a network interface card.
- Connecting the card to the workstation and network.
- Copying network files needed to start the workstation.
- Testing the workstation on the network.

If you are comfortable with installing an entire microcomputer's components—the monitor, keyboard, printer, and other internal peripherals such as modems or memory cards, you should be able to configure a microcomputer as a workstation. If you are unsure about these tasks, you might want to have the systems consultant work through them with you, and then try a few on your own. This way, you will be better prepared for installing a new workstation. You might even request that the systems consultant walk you through the steps in this chapter on the first workstation you install.

Moving a workstation from one location to another is also reviewed. In addition, planning for and testing the new location, preparing the workstation before the move, and installing it in the new location are all discussed. Although this task is relatively straightforward and you may already have done it, you should take time to review the brief process outlined.

If you learn the proper sequence of steps needed to either install a new workstation or move an existing one, it will take you only a short time to perform these tasks with confidence. Knowing how to do this is a big benefit—it saves time, personnel, and money. Users of the network can be up and running immediately, rather than depending on a hardware specialist to find time in his or her schedule. The first step in adding a new workstation to the network is selecting the cable, which is discussed in the next section.

Selecting Cable

One of the first steps in adding a new workstation to your network is determining the type of cable required by the system. Although the process of installing the cable is typically done by the systems consultant, as a systems administrator you should be aware of the type of cable needed for your system. You might find occasion to order new or replacement cable or connection components. Or you could be required to manage the new cable installation by the installer and be asked to provide the correct type of cable. In most cases, use of the incorrect cable will result in major problems such as poor performance or inability to connect.

The type of network interface card (NIC) determines the type of cable used. You should have identified the NIC your system uses in Part I using the CONFIG program on the file server. Your systems installer should have noted the type of cable; also most cable installers should be able to tell you what type of cable is used. An incorrect match in cabling will cause problems, so you should take great care in ensuring the proper match.

Various types of cable include telephone wire, twisted pair, shielded, coax, fiber optic, or baseband. The cable can be attached to connection devices such as repeaters (devices that extend the cable length beyond its normal limit), hubs (electrical devices to which file server cable and numerous workstations are attached), wire centers (used similar to hubs on token-passing ring networks), and terminator devices (used on the last workstation on the network).

Your network may use one or more type of cable if you are bridging two or more networks of varying topology. You should also locate repeaters, hubs, wire centers (on token passing ring systems), and last workstation on the network. Complete the form in Figure 5.1 for each network with your systems consultant.

Once you have determined the cable requirements for the new workstation, arrange the installation process. If the cable is already in place, you need only configure and install the network card and attach the new workstation. The next section discusses setting up the various network cards supported by NetWare.

Configuring the Network Interface Card (NIC)

The next step in adding a new workstation on the network is to set or configure the network interface card properly for your system. There are several types of cards supported by Novell. Table 5.1 shows each type and the various settings you need to consider. There are five basic terms used in setting an NIC:

- IRQ interrupt jumper.
- I/O base memory address.
- Station address.
- DMA.
- Connector type (thick or thin).

Type of NIC: ________

Type of cable: ________

Connection devices: Enter number of each on network

Repeater 1 _____ Repeater 2 _____ Repeater 3 _____ Repeater 4 _____
Location _____ Location _____ Location _____ Location _____

_____ Wire center (complete chart below for each)

Receptacle	Ring In	1	2	3	4	5	6	7	8	Ring Out
Connect to										
Workstation										

_____ Passive hub (complete chart below for each)

Receptacle	1	2	3	4
Connect to				
Workstation				

_____ Active hub (complete chart below for each)

Receptacle	1	2	3	4	5	6	7	8
Connect to								
Workstation								
or Hub								

_____ MAU (Multistation Active Unit) (complete chart below for each)

Receptacle	Ring In	1	2	3	4	5	6	7	8	Ring Out
Connect to										
Workstation										

Location of last workstation on network ________________________
Terminator type (optional on certain networks): __________________

Figure 5.1 Workstation cabling information.

If you have little familiarity with this terminology, don't worry. Each card's configuration requirements are different and are easy to set using the accompanying NIC manual. You may only need to set two of the five settings. For example, only one group of cards uses the connector type setting.

These settings are simple to change and employ either a *dip-switch block*, a small set of plastic levers that slide to an off or on position, or a *jumper pin*, a removable piece of plastic with holes that fits around different sets of pins attached to the network interface card. These two devices are typically used in memory adaptors and other peripherals that require settings. Most network interface cards are factory set, except for those that require a unique station address. This address is usually a number from 1 to 256 and can be set by using a combination of dip-switches. Complete guides for each card's station addresses are found in the accompanying manual that also explains its setting requirements.

Table 5.1 Setting Options for NICs Supported by NetWare

Setting	NIC model/ and PC adaptor	IBM TRN/A Proteon
IRQ interrupt jumper	yes	yes
I/O base memory address	yes	yes
Station address	no	yes
DMA	no	yes
Connector type (thin or thick)	no	no

NIC model/ Setting	Arcnet Rx-net	Ethernet 3-Com, Orchid G-Net
IRQ interrupt jumper	yes	yes
I/O base memory address	yes	yes
Station address	yes	no
DMA	no	no
Connector or cable type (thin or thick)	no	yes

Note: Since the S-Net dedicated file server has a specially designed adaptor card, and its workstations already contain factory preset network interface cards, the above settings are not needed and documentation is unnecessary.

Once you have set a station address for the Arcnet, Rx-net, or Proteon cards, mark it on the back of each card and create a master list for your network as shown in Figure 5.2.

Once you have properly configured the network card, it is ready to install in the microcomputer to be used as a workstation.

Workstation Identifier Master Listing
Company ________
As of __/__/__

Identifier	Station Address	Physical Address	Serial No	Location/User Name
AF-1	33	1F	123456789	ACCOUNTING-MARY
PC-1	255	FF	987654321	EXECUTIVE-TOM
XT-1	254	FE	135792468	ANALYST-PAT

Figure 5.2 Station address listing.

Installing the Network Interface Card (NIC)

To install the NIC into the microcomputer, first review its installation manual. Each card's manual provides easy step-by-step instructions for installation. Next, remove the cover from the computer system unit using a screwdriver. Select an empty long or short expansion slot depending on the size of the NIC. If it is short, use a short slot if available since many other expansion cards often require a long slot. Remove the protective plate that opens to the back of the unit from the slot you select. Insert the card carefully following the instructions that are included. Attach the card to the workstation securely using the screw provided. A card improperly fastened can become unseated easily and result in a disconnection from the network. Replace the cover on the computer system unit.

Once you have attached the card to the workstation, you are ready to attach the workstation to the network.

Attaching the Workstation to the Network

Once again you must make sure the installed cable type is correct. At the end of the cable is a metal connector that attachs to the NIC. Connect it to the plug of the NIC—some cables need to be turned slightly to firmly attach them. Make sure the other end of the cable is connected to the network via a hub, wire center, existing workstation, or directly to the server. No software settings are required to add a new workstation on the server.

Note: The Network Assistant program requires the new workstation's Physical Workstation ID, which can be found using the SESSION program menu. This process is discussed in Part I.

Copying Network Start-Up Files onto the Workstation

Before you can test the new workstaton on the network, you will need a boot disk or a set of files copied to the computer's hard disk. Using DOS, copy the shell program from an identical existing workstation boot disk. It should contain an IPX and ANETx or NETx file depending on:

- IPX.COM (NetWare Version 2.1x above);
- ANETx.com (NetWare Versions 2.0a and below); or
- NETx.com (NetWare Versions 2.1 and above).
  (x is DOS version of workstation boot disk).

It may also contain the following files:

- NETBIOS.EXE (optional; depends on software).
- INT2F.com (required with NETBIOS applications).

These should be entered into an AUTOEXEC.BAT file using the COPY CON command, the EDLIN utility, or a text editor program. If you are using a boot disk, it must be formatted with the /S option and contain the DOS file COMMAND.COM.

A typical AUTOEXEC.BAT file for a workstation using NetWare Version 2.1 or above and DOS 3.x (that runs an application requiring NETBIOS) looks like:

```
echo off

prompt $p$g

ipx

netbios

int2F
```

```
net3
f:
login
```

Note: NetWare Version 2.0a does not use the **ipx** statment. The **net3** statement is replaced with **anetx**, depending on DOS level.

If your application does not require NETBIOS, eliminate the **netbios** and **int2F** statements.

To generate these files for a workstation using a new level of DOS, ask your systems consultant to create the workstation shell files for it using the SHGEN diskettes. He or she should also modify the appropriate server directory to include the necessary new DOS version files. For more on network shell files, see "Shells" in Chapter 4.

Testing the Workstation on the Network

To test the workstation, insert the boot diskette and turn the power on. If it has a hard disk, you only need to turn the power on. If the physical connection is valid, the message appears on screen:

```
Attached to server SERVERNAME, at date/time.
```

If this message does not appear and the system does not respond with a message, or a message such as "File server not found" appears, check to see if the:

- File server is powered up.
- Cable is damaged.
- Cables are properly connected.
- Workstation NIC station address is unique.
- Workstation NIC has a malfunction.

Try connecting the new workstation to a cable used on an existing workstation that you know functions. If it does attach, either the other cable is damaged or improperly connected. If it does NOT attach, most likely the NIC is damaged or not set properly.

If the system displays the message:

```
Bad command or filename
```

check for the following: shell files are appropriate for the DOS level, command lines are typed correctly, shell files are resident on the boot disk.

Once the workstation is attached, you will have access to the file server for login. To do this, type

```
F: [Enter]
LOGIN login name [Enter]
password (if assigned) [Enter]
```

If it's not already in the AUTOEXEC.BAT file, you can include **F:** and **login** as shown previously.

You have now learned the steps needed to install a new workstation. It is a good idea to have your systems consultant show you how to set up your first new workstation on your network. Now that you have the basics for installing a workstation, you can see how easy it is to move a workstation.

Moving a Workstation

Often you will be asked to move a workstation to a new location. An employee may move to another office, one employee may need more resources and wish to trade with another, or your entire department may need to move to another office. The steps in moving a workstation are:

1. Plan the new cable to the new location; arrange for installation.
2. Test the cable in the new location with another workstation to keep move time to a minimum.
3. Make sure to back up any hard disk files and park the hard disk if possible using DOS.
4. Disconnect the cable from the NIC on the back of the workstation and all other cables (monitor, keyboard, printer, modem).
5. Move the workstation to the new location. If your type of cable system requires that the cable end be terminated, attach the proper device to the cable end if you do not plan to use it for another workstation.
6. Attach the cable to the NIC on the workstation; plug in the workstation, including the monitor, printer, and keyboard.
   - Test the workstation with the boot disk.
   - Attach any other peripherals to the system.
   - Update the new location in the system documentation.

Whether moving or adding a workstation to the network, you should consider installing surge protectors. Part I discusses backup media, uninterruptable and standby power supplies, and surge protectors used for networks.

Summary

In this chapter you have learned how to add a new workstation to the network using basic procedures—identifying cable and NIC type, NIC configuration, and physical installation. We have also discussed considerations and procedures for moving workstations. The next chapter discusses connectivity from a microcomputer without a network interface card using only a modem to connect to your NetWare network.

Chapter 6

Connecting a Remote Workstation to a Network

Many users have a computer at home, work in an office without the file server, or travel on the road. They could use access to the file server, but do not know how to set it up. The procedure to connect a microcomputer offsite or *remote* to a network is not always obvious. This next section illustrates the easiest of the methods available. You only need to install two modems, two copies of a communications program—and you can have worldwide access to your file server and its valuable data 24 hours a day.

You should be familiar enough with the microcomputer hardware you are using to be able to install a peripheral into its expansion slots or externally to a serial port address (known as COM1 or COM2). Be sure to determine the address of the serial port before beginning this task.

Connecting Via a Modem

There are various ways to connect a remote microcomputer without a network interface card to an existing network, but we will present the easiest in this chapter—using a workstation attached to the network (booted up with the shell program) with one modem attached and no other special hardware. The remote microcomputer must have a modem and should use the same communications program as the network workstation. This program must provide *emulation* or the ability for the remote to function identical to the network workstation. Programs we recommend for emulation are:

NetWare AnyWare
Manufacturer: Novell, Inc.
Address: 122 East 1700 South
Provo, UT 84606
Telephone: (801) 379-5900 (800) LAN-KIND
Retail Price: $395
Note: One software license includes both the host and remote software.

Carbon Copy Plus, Version 5.1
Manufacturer: Microcom Software
Address: 500 River Ridge Drive
Norwood, MA 02062
Telephone: (800) 822-8224
Retail Price: $195 (versions are unique based on serial number and contain both a support and remote option: Two copies must be purchased for a complete installation).

Close Up
Manufacturer: Norton-Lambert
Address:
Telephone:
Retail Price: customer version, $195; support version, $245.

Remote 2
Manufacturer: DCA
Address:
Telephone:
Retail Price: $195 (host and caller version).

All of these programs require the network workstation to be attached to the network with the shell. Login should be done from the remote microcomputer in order to assure security. We recommend that you leave this computer as a dedicated receiver; that will not allow users to do work during the hours you expect to access it. The model of this workstation can be an older type such as an IBM PC or XT with an 8088-based CPU because the faster CPU does not increase performance.

Setting Up the Communication Software and Modems

For the programs Carbon Copy Plus, Close Up, and Remote 2, both the remote and workstation should have the same communications programs with unique versions installed. You need a customer or caller or different serial number version for one station and a support or host version for the other. Take care in keeping track of which version is which while installing. Standardizing your communications using either of these three programs makes the procedure easier to learn and support.

If you require support from users calling in with a variety of communications programs, the NetWare Anywhere program provides the best type of connection. A user dials in with one of the supported communications software programs and NetWare Anywhere answers, regardless of the program used to dial.

Each computer's modem must have identical speed capabilities. Set each modem to the same speed using either a switch on the modem or the communications software. Speed is usually set during the communications program's installation procedure. Other installation settings include selecting the correct COM port where the modem is connected—either COM1 or COM2 for most computers.

You then attach each computer's modem to the phone line. You should know whether the phone line is a touch-tone or the pulse dial type and its number before attempting to make a connection.

Successful communication depends on setting *protocol*, or special communications parameters, identically for each computer using the program you have selected. Most users don't understand these settings; you need not concern yourself with their meaning. You should, however, note that baud rate is the speed at which the data travels via the modem. It may be set during installation. These other basic settings are usually set once the program has been invoked:

- Parity (odd, none, or even).
- Baud rate (300, 1200, 2400 or higher).
- Stop bits (1 or 0).
- Word length (7 or 8).
- Duplex (full or half).

They can usually be saved to disk once set. Check your communications manual for this feature.

All the packages support a *null modem*, or a simple cable run directly between two microcomputers located near each other. For example, if you have a computer in one office with a network interface card and you want to connect it to another located in the next office, you can install a cable between the two and install each program with the NO MODEM setting. See the reference manual for more on this procedure. This is particularly useful if the hardware of one computer is not compatible with a network interface card, such as expanded memory, VGA graphics cards and other peripherals that demand memory addresses that conflict with a network interface card memory setting utilized by NetWare Version 2.0x. NetWare Version 2.1 and above users should not have this problem.

Testing the Modems

If you have not used the modem, you should test dial it by dialing any phone number. You should hear the number dial and the phone ring. For more on testing your individual modem, see its reference manual.

If the modem does not dial, check to see if the port has been correctly set, the cables are attached, and if you have specified the correct type of phone line—either pulse or touch-tone. These are some examples of common mistakes. Check with your systems consultant or vendor for additional support.

The next section will show step-by-step how to use Carbon Copy Version 5.1, a communications program used to connect a remote microcomputer to a NetWare network.

Connecting to a Network from a Remote Microcomputer with Carbon Copy Plus

Using Carbon Copy Plus Version 5.1 involves performing a few basic tasks. You must purchase two copies, one for the network workstation, or *host*, and one for the remote microcomputer, or *local*. Next, you install each copy on each computer and set the port, baud rate, and call table for each modem. Finally, you set the network workstation to receive as the host using the CC program; the remote or local will use the CCHELP program to dial it up. The following sections show the necessary steps for each of these tasks.

If you are using another program, these same basic tasks should apply. Check your manual for specifics on installation and configuration, setting the network to receive and making the connection from the remote.

Installing Carbon Copy Plus

To install Carbon Copy Plus, create a directory called CC on the hard disk on both the network workstation with the modem and the remote microcomputer. Load one Carbon Copy Plus master program disk in the floppy drive of the first computer and type at the A> prompt:

```
CCSTART [Enter]
```

This program prompts you to fill out a sign-on screen with your company name and creates the files CCHELP and CC on the master disk. You will then be asked to install the program for your screen, modem type, and modem port. The details of running the CCINSTAL program follow this section. Next copy the files to the directory CC from the master floppy and utility disks. Make sure to note the serial number of the program used for each computer. You cannot install the Carbon Copy Plus program files with one serial number on another computer and use that computer to connect to the original.

Run the install program for each to verify baud and COM port on both computers and set frequently used telephone numbers on disk in the call table.

To run the install program,

TYPE/PRESS	RESULT:
ccinstal[Enter]	Checks to see if settings are correct for COM port, baud rate, modem type, or system type.

You will press the letter to change the setting and continue pressing it until the correct setting appears.

A	Changes Com port address to COM1, COM2, COM3, or COM4.
B	Changes Baud Rate to 300, 600, 1200, 2400, 4800, 9600, or 19.2k.
C	Presents a menu of modem types to select from.
D	Changes System type to IBM compatible, Compaq 286, or IBM.
E and F	Change screen type and menu colors.
G	Changes Default directory.
1	Sets common optional parameters (not required).
2	Presents a table where you can store frequently dialed telephone numbers frequently dialed (you should enter the telephone number of the network workstation's modem line here for the remote microcomputer).
3	Sets passwords for the program (defaults to CC unless set).

To save the changes you make, press X. To exit the install menu without changes saved, press Q. You will be prompted to confirm the exit with a Yes or No prompt.

You are now ready to set the network workstation to receive and access it from the remote microcomputer.

Setting the Network Workstation Modem to Receive

o use a workstation to connect to the remote microcomputer, use the program CC that is included with Carbon Copy Plus. First make sure the server is powered up. Next boot the network workstation with the modem. It must be attached to the network via the shell (for more on loading the shell, see "Shells" in Chapter 4).

To set it to receive

TYPE/PRESS	RESULT:
c:[Enter]	Changes current drive to C
cd \ cc [Enter]	Changes directory to CC (assume this is the location of Carbon Copy Plus)
cc [Enter]	Loads the Carbon Copy Plus CC program

The workstation should be displaying the Carbon Copy Plus menu shown in Figure 6.1. You must leave this workstation active in this menu to make the connection. However, you may want to turn the monitor intensity to low or completely off so that the characters do not burn an image into the screen. Or there are screen saving programs that wait 15 seconds or so for keyboard input and blank the screen. Make sure you leave a sign on the keyboard that the computer is in use and should not be powered off.

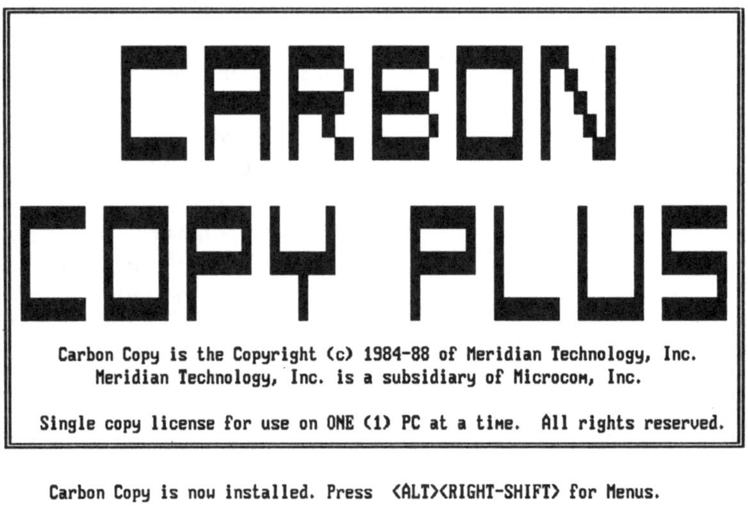

Figure 6.1 Carbon Copy Plus CC menu.

Note: If you are using a hard disk to run Carbon Copy Plus, insert the command REMOTE either at the end of the AUTOEXEC.BAT file on the network workstation or type at the DOS prompt.

Enter the commands into a file named REMOTE.BAT as

```
c:
cd\cc
cc
```

Note: If you are using a floppy disk to run Carbon Copy, insert the command REMOTE either at the end of the AUTOEXEC.BAT file on the boot disk or type at the DOS A> prompt.

Enter the commands into a file named REMOTE.BAT on the boot disk as

```
a:
cd\cc
cc
```

You are now ready to connect a user on a remote microcomputer to the workstation and the network.

Dialing the Network

To connect the remote microcomputer to the network, you use the other connection program that is included with Carbon Copy Plus called CCHELP. This program assigns the computer the status of *local* and the computer you are calling *host*. To make a connection from a local to a host, first power up the remote microcomputer and the modem. Next load the Carbon Copy software and dial the network workstation:

TYPE/PRESS	RESULT:
c: [Enter]	Changes drive to C
cd \cc [Enter]	Changes directory to CC (Carbon Copy program)
cchelp [Enter]	Loads the Carbon Copy support program CCHELP
F1	Calls the CC User network workstation
highlight name from CALL Table on left box	Selects network workstation number to dial
[Enter]	Dials the number

CC [Enter]	Enters the default password and completes the connection
F: [Enter]	Makes remote drive F current

Your screen should look like the network workstation's and your network's F> prompt should appear on screen. You are now ready to log into the network. Type:

Login username [Enter]
Password (if required) [Enter]

You now have the same access as you would on the network from a workstation. To change the drive or directory, type the letter and press [Enter].

The next section shows how to copy a file from your remote microcomputer to the network workstation.

Copying a File from the Local (Remote) to the Host (Network Workstation)

Once you have activated the connection between the local and host, your screen appears to only have access to the other computer's drives and directories. The C> prompt will display the network workstation's C drive and so forth for A> or B>. However, it is only a "carbon copy" of the host's resources. You still have access to your original remote or local computer's drives. To access those drives to copy files to or from the network, you must return to the Carbon Copy Plus menu and use the File Transfer program.

For example, suppose you want to copy a file on your local drive to the file server directory in order for another network user to have access. You change the host drive to the target directory to make sure you have it mapped correctly (if you need to review mapping, see "Mapping a Logical Drive or Search Directory" in Chapter 4). Once you are sure you have access, you are ready to copy the local file to that file server directory. You can even access the host computer's local drive C. The same DOS COPY command is used, but instead you insert L or H in front of the drive: \ directory \ filename you want to copy.

To copy a file from a local drive C to a host drive F from a connection to the file server (you should have connected using the steps from the previous section and have a host drive as the current drive), type

TYPE/PRESS	RESULT:
Alt-Shift	Displays the Carbon Copy Plus menu

Note: Use the Shift key located on the right side of the keyboard (referred to as the right-Shift by Carbon Copy).

F5	Selects the File Transfer program

copy LC:path \ filename HF:path \ filename [Enter]

	Copies file from local drive to host or network drive F

Note: The time for the file copying process depends on the speed of the modem and file size in bytes. A small status graph will display the percent copied on screen.

exit [Enter]	Returns to Carbon Copy Plus menu
F10	Returns to displaying drive and current directory (prior to copying file)

The file transfer program is a handy way to upload and download files to and from the file server.

Summary

This chapter has touched briefly on the various programs you can use to connect a remote microcomputer to a NetWare network. It has shown the basic steps for setting up the modem hardware, testing it, and making the actual connection with it. Carbon Copy Plus Version 5.1, a popular program that is used to connect via modems, has been used to show step-by-step instructions for connecting a remote to the network. The actual program includes many other features that include a simple to use file transfer program for exchanging files to and from the network as well as local or host computer drive systems. With this basic information, you should be able to connect remotely to your NetWare network anytime or any place.

Appendix A

Authorized Education Centers

The Novell Authorized Education Center (NAEC) is designed to provide educational resources for NetWare users and resellers. NAECs offer NetWare users the quality training they demand with the recognititon of having certified NetWare instructors on staff. Novell works hand-in-hand with NAECs to maintain the reputation of the logo.

1. NAEC instructors continuously attend update training from Novell.
2. NAECs give customer satisfaction guarantees to their students.
3. NAECs are audited by Novell to insure a quality educational program.
4. NOVELL published student kits are used only at NAECs.
5. NAECs limit class size so students receive individualized instruction.
6. Certified NetWare Instructors (CNI) are the only instructors NAECs use.

Register for your NOVELL training at an NAEC near you:

ALASKA
TCBC CompuEaze
Anchorage
(907) 561-4677/(800) 478-4677

CALIFORNIA
Interconnect Network
Consulting Group, Inc.
Pasadena
(818) 796-9787/(800) LANS-R-US

CONNECTICUT
HBM Business Education Center
Hartford
(203) 243-1000/(413) 788-4659

ILLINOIS
ODC Systems
Chicago
(800) 325-LANS

INDIANA
BBM Office Products
Bloomington
(812) 333-5226

KENTUCKY
Micro Computer Solutions, Inc.
Louisville
(800) 456-3005/(502) 499-8260

MINNESOTA
Connect Computer Company
Minneapolis
(612) 944-0181

NEW JERSEY
Alared Consulting Services, Inc.
Brick
(800) ALARED1

NEW YORK
Westcon Systems Corp.
New York City
(212) 465-9000

NORTH CAROLINA
Cedalion System, Inc.
Charlotte/RTP
(704) 335-1200/(919) 549-8116

OHIO
CBM Systems
Columbus
(800) 288-5937/(614) 488-5937

OREGON
Pacific Dataware, Inc.
Lake Oswego/Portland
(800) 234-4734

PENNSYLVANIA
The MATRIX Organization
King of Prussia
(215) 293-1980

TEXAS
Business Systems Group
Houston
(800) 950-5267
Informa, Inc.
Austin
(512)338-4499

WASHINGTON
Paragon Computer Corp.
Redmond
(206) 562-0500

WASHINGTON D.C., MARYLAND
HTR, Inc.
Rockville
(301) 881-6420

PUERTO RICO
Diaz, Rosario & Co.
Puerto Nuevo
(809) 792-9480
Instruction in Spanish and English

Appendix B

Forms for System Documentation

Table of Contents

Systems Documentation

Form A-1 File Server Inventory

File Server Purpose	NetWare Name	Location	Model

Form A-2 Hardware configuration information for file server

Number of service Processes: [ ]

LAN A Configuration information:
Network Address: [ ] [ ]
Hardware Type: [ ]
Hardware Settings: IRQ =[ ] I/O Base = [ ]
RAM Buffer at [ ]

Form A-5 Network printer configuration

Printer Model/Name	Location	Port/Number

Form A-6 Workstation inventory

Company ______________________________ As of: __/__/__

Identifier tag—type/number		
Station Address		
Physical Address (via SESSION)		
Serial Number		
Location/User		
User Name		

Hardware related:
- Manufacturer ______________________________
- Hard disk size______________________________
  - Free space______________________________
  - Manufacturer______________________________
- Conventional RAM memory______________________________
- Add-on memory______________________________
- Clock/Calendar______________________________
- Display type______________________________
- Printer (local)______________________________
- Ports - parallel______________________________
  - - serial______________________________
- Modem type/speed______________________________
  - Internal/External______________________________
  - COM1 or COM2 port______________________________
- Keyboard type______________________________

Floppy disk drives______________________________

Software related:______________________________
- Network boot disk operating system/version______________________________
  - Shell files______________________________
  - CONFIG.SYS special parameters______________________________
  - AUTOEXEC.BAT______________________________

Directory/name/serial #________________________________
stand-alone software________________________________
on local hard disk________________________________
Word processing________________________________

Spreadsheet________________________________

Database________________________________

Communications________________________________

Graphics________________________________

Other________________________________

Form A-7 Workstation identifiers

Workstation Identifier Master Listing
Company ________
As of __/__/__

Identifier	Station Address	Physical Address	Serial No	Location/User Name

Form A-8 File server directory structure

Directory	Subdirectory	Subdirectory

Index

A

D

E

F

J

K

L

M

N

O

P

Q

R

S

T

U

V

W

About the Author

Carolyn Jane Jorgensen was born and raised in Illinois, where she attended the University of Illinois at Champaign, and received her B.S. in business administration.. She accredits her early success in computer consulting and training to that environment. Upon graduation she headed West to embark on what she hoped was a career in international business.

Following a six month break in Australia and the Orient, she returned to San Francisco in 1981, where she worked for Bechtel Corporation as a financial analyst. Her chief duty was compiling the mainframe-based computer analysis for quarterly investment reports.

In 1983 she started her company, Micro Touch Computer Training, in San Francisco. Fluent in Spanish, Portugese, and French, she had little trouble teaching Lotus 1-2-3 to her clients. She signed her first book contract that summer and has since published several books on Lotus 1-2-3 and Symphony. Many translations have been done of her Lotus 1-2-3 books.

Receiving her M.B.A. in 1987, she continued to work with large and small Bay Area businesses, supporting their users in the operation of local area networks. She currently lives 60 miles north of San Francisco in Santa Rosa, with her husband, Gilles.